SEX IS HARD WORK

EMILY PAYNE

CHAPTERS

CHAPTER 1

I DON'T KNOW WHAT ELSE TO DO!

Hello readers, I'm Emily, and I'm a prostitute. I was thirty-three when this story started, fourteen years ago. I had been coming and going from jobs every few months, or every couple of years since I left school at 16. I just got bored with the jobs, always thinking the grass was greener.

After seventeen years of this, I was frustrated and searching for a solution. I had tried loads of different jobs, but always hated them and, let's face it, they take up so much of your day, don't they?! I wasn't getting any younger and contemplating my future. I was sick of working boring repetitive nine-to-fives, which left me exhausted in the evenings and just catching up on housework and washing at the weekends. To sum up, 9 to 5 jobs; -destroying souls for next to no financial benefit since the beginning of time!

I had also tried out a couple of business ideas too, but with no success. It was all quite depressing and was making me increasingly sad and angry. There must have been another way.

I had dabbled in working for phone sex chat lines before but had given up when I simply ran out of sex crap to chat about! I suppose I could have just done heavy breathing down the receiver but doing that for a prolonged amount of time doesn't half make you light-headed and dehydrated! I did, however, have a sound effects table – my coffee table. Some of the props were a bowl of water, a jug, and a banana. If a caller was into all things 'toilet', I would pour water from the jug into the bowl to simulate weeing and would drop a chunk of banana in to simulate the obvious... a woman's work was never done. Having something to hand with a long zip was another essential, I had many callers who liked to think I was unzipping my clothes for them or zipping up a pair of long kinky boots...I never was!

I was a single woman, with no kids (and still am) that side of life has never interested me, confident and had tried many jobs ranging from the sublime to the ridiculous. I would give anything a go, including working as a life model for art students. I found that holding one position and staring into the middle distance, muse style, for anything over twenty-five minutes REALLY hurt, but I had rent to pay, so I ploughed on.

I had been through probably thirty-five jobs since leaving school (for some I even wore clothes!) before I started escorting. They included working as a professional singer and an amateur burlesque performer. I had never found a job I liked, paid enough, or was prepared to stick to long term. I had moved to London in my early 20s to work for a volunteer charity, got totally sick of that after a few months, and came back home. I started a small, totally unsuccessful second-hand clothes shop at about 19, featuring a, rather grandiosely named 'bric-a-brac department' that consisted of one shelf with general crap/tat on it, gave my sister a good laugh when she saw it and that was about it. I had worked in the fitness industry as an instructor for years, I had been a very fat teen and 20 something and fitness was my salvation, still is, and worked various retail-type jobs, I worked as post woman for a few months, getting my specially made 'big girls' uniform about a week before I packed in, as well as working in the soul-destroying realm of call centre work. I never had a problem getting jobs, I would turn my hand to most things, it was sticking to them that was the issue.

I had moved out of the family home at 18 and had always been fiercely independent and self-reliant. So here I was, not getting any younger, wanting financial freedom, not wanting to be chained to a minimum wage slow death. Something had to be done.

I had thought about escorting a few times but always put it out of my mind as something other women did, not me. Sometimes as I was chatting 'oh-so-sexily' on the chat line, sometimes pretending to be Cheryl Cole due to my Geordie accent and as requested by several callers, usually telling him I was clad in stockings and suspenders and writhing round on my settee feeling oh so horny (as every woman is doing at 2pm of a Thursday afternoon!). I was actually in my pyjamas, steaming some carrots or some such, but as I would learn to my amazement later – and praise the Lord for it too – most straight men believe what they want when it came to women and sex, and they would buy it every time!

One story from that time that stands out was about a caller who became quite regular.

He used to tout an idea he had for a sexually explicit version of Strictly Come Dancing called Strictly Cum Fucking... hmmm If anyone from the BBC is reading this, I do apologise. It basically consisted of the contestants fucking competitively for the regulation one and a half minutes, being observed and judged by various porn stars. The contestants being stark naked at all times, and the finale, I think I recall correctly seemed to consist of a celebratory communal spunk cocktail contributed to by all male contestants and knocked back by all concerned, very festive!

Sometimes, I would imagine actually having to do the things I was talking about with them, and it would turn my stomach. I would be thankful that he was at the end of a phone line. Other times, I would be sitting having a cuppa in a café on a busy high street. I would choose a window seat so I could people watch and would say to myself, 'OK, you have to have sex with all the men that walk past you' and question whether I would be able to. I had always concluded that I couldn't and so had always dismissed the idea of escorting, working on the principle that any of those men could be a client.

But now, my working situation was bearing down on me, coming and going from jobs, working 3 jobs at once and still just getting by, at my age was ridiculous, and I had to make a decision.

This book is about my working life as an escort. There won't be any lurid details from my own sex life (none of your bloody business!), but I think it will be useful to give you a bit of background, sex-wise.

I had experienced quite a varied sex life at this point, a lot of casual sex. I'd had a few threesomes, foursomes and I'm sure there was a fivesome tucked in there somewhere. Dress up, role play, sex in strange places, I had done them all and was sexually very confident. I had never had a long-term relationship and sex just didn't mean that much to me – I usually did it in the hope it would be good, but thirty seconds into it I would get that 'wish I'd never bothered' feeling that I'm sure a lot of women recognise! Or I'd just do it to show off, put on a show or do something outrageous to get a reaction. I've always been very open-minded and don't take sex very seriously. If there's something I've wanted to try, I have. I don't ever fret over 'what does this mean? What will people think? Am I a pervert? Am I gay?'; as I find a lot of people do, I just try it.

Most sexual activities are a bit of an anti-climax (excuse the pun) anyway in my book and shouldn't be bothered with twice, or once in a lot of cases, but as I say, this book is not about my own sex life, it's about other people. I was just there at the time!

I was a good-looking woman (I had lost circa five stones in my late 20's) with long black hair, slim but very curvy, average height. I prided myself on my appearance and lived for the gym. I was confident in my looks and wasn't shy about getting my kit off for just about anyone – as I think you will have gathered by now, so that side of things wasn't going to be a problem for me.

I have always been more comfortable with 'weird' situations and people. Situations that freak most people out, I am comfortable with, I find. It's uber normality that I can't deal with, makes me at once nervy and yet bored, odd mix I know, and I have always been very practical, if there's a dirty job to do, I will be the one to do it.

The sticking point was whether I could be sexual with any man just because he had the right amount of cash in his wallet. A friend once annoyed me when, on telling her I had become an escort, said 'well I suppose it's like what you have been doing anyway, isn't it?', referring to my wild and free sex life. I explained to her that no matter how many people I'd had sex with, they had been MY choice, for whatever reason I had chosen them. When escorting, the partners are not your choice and money is involved which, as I'm sure you will agree, changes the dynamics of any relationship or situation in general, and thereby hangs my tale!

I had contacted an escort agency a couple of years before, but I actually started work at a different one. I had spoken with someone about the job and was invited to a photo shoot but bottled it at the last minute. Prostitution was too much of a leap for me at that point, wasn't the right time. It was something other people did, not me. I didn't want that on my life CV, it seemed too weird for want of a better word, I suppose.

But a couple of years later, I had just had enough of my working situation. I was tired and I decided to give it a go, on the understanding that if I did even just one job and didn't want to do another I didn't have to, but at least I could then put it out of my mind as a money maker once and for all. That seemed sensible to me, but if I could have done anything else for the same money and freedom I would have. Although you probably wouldn't have bought a book on the subject, would you?

I started by Googling local escort agencies, but with zero experience in the field, I felt a bit lost. I didn't know a good agency from a bad one. How did they work? What should I be looking for? As I researched, I started to get the measure of some of the agencies and their standards. For example, if the women in the profile pictures were sitting with their house coats half open in front of a radiator with their washing drying on it, including greying bras and green socks, the agency wasn't a good one.

As I trawled through these sites full of very improbably named women – Roxy, Eden, Vixen, and the surprisingly popular Vivian (is that Julia Roberts' character name from 'Pretty Woman', maybe!?), I decided to base my decision on the quality of the photographs of the escorts and which agency was asking for the highest rates; there didn't seem to be anything else to base my decision on. The one I decided on had clearly professional standard photography – the girls were all wearing glamorous underwear, in complimentary poses, faces blurred for privacy and the rates were good.

So, I filled in the online application, attaching a cheeky nude photo – not sure one was asked for but, I'll get my kit off at the drop of a hat in the right situation.

I think it was the next day I got a call from the owner of the agency; he had liked my application. We chatted quite informally for a few minutes, I think he was making sure I knew exactly what the job was, or maybe the naked selfie I had sent was enough to show I did. I was invited for an interview and a photo shoot – if I decided to go ahead with the job. It was in a couple of days' time. He had sounded nice, business-like but friendly and left me feeling relaxed about meeting him.

I don't remember having any doubts or second thoughts over the next couple of days. I had thought my decision through a million times, so I just wanted to get started now – get it over with, if you like.

On the day of the interview, at 1pm, I was driving to meet the man I had spoken to on the phone and that's the only time I had a doubt. I remember getting about five minutes away and being very tempted to turn the car around and forget all about it. But I knew that this was just a last-minute wobble and should be ignored – I'm only human after all, dear reader.

For my interview, I wore a black and pink knee-length dress and black high heel boots, just what I would wear day to day, escort interview or not.

I found a parking space and walked to the flat, pressed the buzzer and the man I had spoken to on the phone answered and let me in, giving me the flat number. I got out of the lift and knocked on the door.

The man answered, smiling, and invited me in. I wasn't scared or intimidated. Speaking to some escorts I eventually got to know, they had been shaking with nerves at their interview and photo shoot. Takes a lot to scare me, which definitely stood me in good stead in my future as an escort. Some people's sexual fantasies and peccadilloes are enough to give anyone the fear!

I walked into a clean, pleasant – if a little sparse and basic – flat, no homely touches: this flat was for seeing clients, I had worked out straight away and who needs scatter cushions and pot pourri just to have sex?

He wanted to know about me in general, rather than a formal interview. We got on very well, I liked him, and he wasn't perving (much), so that was heartening. We spent a couple of hours just talking and laughing.

He told me how the agency ran, the 'practicalities' if you like and I asked questions, although don't ask me what they were, it was years ago – although I'm sure if I could eavesdrop on our conversation now, I would laugh at what would come over now as naivety – how sweet!

Next was the photo shoot. I had brought a small collection of sexy undies, as requested by Steve. Stockings, suspenders, bra, and knicker sets (mainly from ASDA – as it turns out one of the escort's favourite underwear suppliers), fuck me heels and God knows what else. I'm sure I remember taking a kimono for some reason, maybe a subliminal geisha thing, who knows?

Steve told me that he had professional photography experience, so he was going to take the photos. His knowledge and photographic equipment did seem to back this up.

I wasn't apprehensive about having my photograph taken. I chose my first skimpy outfit; I think it involved something crotchless recently acquired from Anne Summers. I wasn't shy posing for half-naked pictures, but it was, however, something new.

Posing in a glamour model style was a first for me and I felt a little awkward and stilted, very unsexy, but the boss knew his stuff, having taken many a sexy pic and I did notice him having to 'rearrange' his crotch a few times, so my posing was having the desired effect on at least one man! This didn't bother me – I couldn't expect to get my substantial boobs out in front of a straight man and for him not to have some rearranging to do, could I?

In some of the poses, I remember feeling quite comical and like I'd been stricken by a strange rictus but hey, what did I know? The pictures turned out very well. The more twisted the pose – the better the sexy photograph apparently.

At this agency, we escorts would be summoned to a photoshoot every six months or so and I got savvier as to what poses and lingerie worked best in photographs to sell my arse online!

After the shoot, Steve asked me when I wanted to start and as I just wanted to make my mind up about it once and for all, I said I would start that night. He said he would upload my profile to the agency website straight away. He would text me with an 'escort name', the false name I would be known as by clients and escorts alike – it's best not to let anyone know anything about you, Steve explained, including the other escorts, which would later prove to be sound advice. I said my goodbyes to Steve and waited for my first job as an escort!

I had told Steve I would work until 2am, which was the latest any of the escorts could work at that agency. He must have set about writing my profile and blurring my face out in my pictures because he quickly texted me a new name, 'Katie', which seemed very pedestrian compared to the Vixens of this world, but I don't think I could have, in all seriousness, answered to the name Vixen – or Vivien for that matter!

At about 10pm he texted me a job; it was an in-call (at one of the agency flats in town, as opposed to an out-call, which meant going to see the client in their home, hotel, or even workplace.). The text contained the time, duration, location, and client's name.

I got in my car and headed to town; not nervous, as I know a lot of new escorts were on their first job – I was more concerned whether I would be able to do it and therefore sort out my need to ditch boring old day jobs once and for all (or until I got too old anyway!).

Within half an hour, I was outside the flat Steve had directed me to. I let myself in; the work flats being left open at all times – and I was in a very small, smart, clean, and tidy flat, similar to my interview venue.

I had dressed appropriately for the job at home beforehand, so I simply titivated my hair and make-up and sat and waited for the buzzer and for the whole thing to get started!

My client's name was Jim. It's funny, but I can remember a lot of my clients from my first few weeks – names, occupations, how sweaty they got! However, after I had been an escort for a few months I couldn't remember anyone.

I remember I had crazily opted to wear thigh-high, fitted boots for the job; very impractical and inflexible – ever tried bending your knees (a 'must-have' ability for a jobbing escort) in tight, over-the-knee boots?

Jim was on time; he buzzed up. I spoke into the intercom and asked his name, to check it wasn't just a drunk who happened to be walking past. It wasn't, and so I pressed the button to open the main door for him (these types of security door flats are vital for a working arrangement).

Jim was late 20s, tall, with dark hair, a bit chubby, clean, and very polite and as it turned out from my hometown; I could have given him a lift if I'd known! Hmm, looked easy I thought, nothing too objectionable here. There was small talk and bullshit. He seemed nervous, whereas I wasn't really. Once he stopped talking about the TV show 'Top Gear', we got on to the subject of what he was after, what kind of experience? He went on to describe what I would later learn was a 'GFE' or 'girlfriend experience'. Which is as it sounds really: kissing, foreplay, sex, and chit-chat. Later in my career, I would sometimes joke with the client and ask if they would like an argument thrown in, as couples seem to specialise in them and that seemed more 'girlfriendy' to me.

The sex must have been very non-descript and easy because I cannot remember it. He didn't have any 'needs' other than the usual, i.e., the thought that an attractive woman wanted him (it's shame you men really are a slave to that one!).

It was then that I realised escorting was the only acting

job the actress wasn't going to win an Oscar for, although there should definitely have been 'The Escort Oscars'. I'd love to have seen the goodie bag! As an escort, you are generally full of BS from the minute your client walks in until the minute you close the front door on them. That's what makes a good escort, Oscar-winning acting skills...and a strong stomach, but that wasn't necessary for good old Jim – all very basic, thank God.

I have heard of new escorts first jobs being weird in some way. There was one whose client had requested she sit on a 'male' blow-up doll and simulate sex, which she did, but then heard a loud bang and Mr. Plastic had burst! No dignity there for that poor young woman, no dignity, but a good story to tell her grandchildren... maybe.

Or the escort who had to do something creative in a gas mask, it was all very 'Dad's Army', I'm sure. Anyway, Jim and I chatted about something and nothing after the sex. I'd been surreptitiously checking my watch through the last twenty minutes of the appointment and, five minutes to the hour, I told him his time was almost up and we dressed then I walked him to the door. I had not been nervous, and it had all been very easy actually but then again, he was a model first client, I'd been lucky.

Later that week, I worked again; my second client was a different affair. Again, it was an in-call and in the same flat. I can't recall his name, but he was around sixty-five, I would say – a lot older than any man I had ever had sex with, and I would ever consider having sex with. He was polite but I felt this was quite a thin veneer and he creeped me out a bit – nothing that he was actually doing wrong, as it were, but he just creeped me out. I had kissed Jim as it had seemed important to him (and I was new to the job!) and as he was more like someone I might actually have sex with, in my real life. It hadn't seemed too 'icky' (and I had checked his mouth for corner spit and rotten teeth), but there was no way that I was going to kiss what I considered to be an old man, I thought.

It's a cliché that prostitutes will have sex with a client but kissing is usually a no-no; this is true I find. Kissing is too up close, and generally something to be kept for the private life. Most escorts offer certain services 'at discretion'. Kissing and anal sex are the main two. This is very important as certain things have to be checked out in person before an escort can make a decision on either. The perils of kissing - rotten mouth, rotten teeth, rancid man breath, mouth with saliva issues. Perils of anal sex – which boils down to erections size and shape. It never fails to amaze me how men with these issues seem totally unaware of them or maybe think as a sex worker I wouldn't mind, like I was no longer a normal woman. Tip to future escorts; do not agree to either of these services', client's unseen, EVER.

Anyway, back to my client. As we had sex, with him behind me, I could feel his sweat dripping on me he had some kind of weird shake – to this day I don't know what that was, but I really endured that appointment, couldn't wait for him to leave.

I was covered in his sweat and saliva after we had sex and just wanted to get into the shower. He hadn't been rude or disrespectful, but I was shaky after that (not as shaky as him though – haha) and I had my first doubts. I didn't feel dirty or shameful, no, it was just a bit of a shock to the system, I suppose – something totally new and different and a big component of it was that it had just been plain gross.

A successful escort must develop a strong gut! I remember texting Steve and telling him I wasn't sure if I could do the work if I was going to feel like that after some jobs. He gave me some platitude or other, saying I had received a good review from Jim on the website and good feedback about my profile, but I knew he was bound to say these things; he was on commission after all. He didn't say I had to work, no pressure and I knew it was a decision I had to make myself.

After a nice cup of tea and a good night's sleep, I decided not to let something a being a bit gross' stop me. It was a wake-up call, that's all, after my relatively easy Mr. Jim experience (I would see Jim a few years later and boy, had his tastes changed. Read on to find out more). I would go on to see dozens of clients like that second one and they wouldn't even register after a few weeks on the job. I had found my strong stomach!

CHAPTER 2

GETTING IN TO THE SWING.

The agency had around thirty women working as escorts, from eighteen years of age to around forty, the vast majority being mid-twenties. So, I was one of the older ones and, as so, felt a little protective towards the younger ones when I first started; later I wouldn't bother!

Some I would bump into a lot and got to know, others didn't work a lot, so I never met them. Most would tell you their real names and chat about their jobs, studies, and kids. Some escorts were more closed. I was incredibly open when I first started, letting other escorts (but never clients) know my name and where I lived. I too would later start to be more secretive and not as friendly toward the other escorts. Not that I was actively unfriendly, but I held back a lot more.

This is a business where people may not be all they seem, and it is a job that in my experience you should keep very separate from your "real life. It can be an underworld that attracts shady or dubious characters, as well as the odd nice, decent person too (me for one!).   I learned over the years to keep my own counsel, and, to work alone, never have anything to do with anyone else in the sex industry, most of whom, I found to be flaky, unprofessional, and well, just weird. I don't feel like I have much in common with other sex workers, other than the occasional lockjaw possibly.

Most escorts do it part-time, having day jobs, studies, and children. It's just a financial necessity for a lot of women. Many of the escorts I met over the years were working to pay off debt – either their own or, sometimes, debt run up by an absent partner. One escort I knew had a crippling shopping addiction, a spare room filled with brand new clothes all still bagged and tagged – although how much they actually paid off is unclear as I found that when most saw the money roll in, they would usually squander it. It would always bemuse me why the other escorts were always broke, considering their earning potential!

Steve, the boss, loved a broke escort; he knew they would be desperate for work all the time! Some escorts did it to finance a shopping addiction, or a buzzing social life. Or, like any job where it's possible to earn oodles of cash, it went up their nose, which I just couldn't fathom, maybe because I don't have and have never had an addiction, but it's a hard job to do just to snort the proceeds. What a waste!

Recruitment would always double whenever there was a new series of 'Secret diary of a call girl' on TV. Seemed to give some women the idea it was a glamorous life. Suppose it is if you find trudging around having sex on many an unwashed duvet cover, glamourous.

A busy, popular escort could earn a few thousand per week, but early on, I decided to just earn a living. I discovered that I absolutely loved the free time this type of work afforded me to pursue other things. I am not acquisitive and don't have expensive tastes. The work was regular, and I always knew I could earn the big bucks if I wanted to and that was a comfort. I'd never dreamed of being rich, just secure and, you may think it sounds weird, but I did feel financially secure. I paid bills and was Little Miss Sensible. I tried a shopping spree once – I came back with one pair of earrings; I'm not cut out for shopping; it bores me to death.

The escorts I was working with ranged from a bit skanky to stunning and it was agency policy not to employ women over dress size 14, but otherwise there was a selection of different looks and 'types', although I did notice there being a higher than the national average (if there is one) of hair extension users, the wiry strands of which festooned the work flats like lametta on a Christmas tree!

The average escort is physically incapable of housework of any kind. We escorts were expected to keep the work flats clean and tidy, but boy did this not happen! I have seen some shocking sights in my time in these flats, dirty girls! It was usually up to a few of the more diligent escorts to angrily and resentfully wield a vacuum cleaner around the place and yes, I was one of them and yes, I am still resentful!

When I first started, and I could still be bothered to talk to the other escorts, we would get talking about why we were doing the job or how we felt about it, some would say they did it because they 'loved sex' which I just thought was total rubbish. Fair enough, love sex as much as you want, but with any Tom, Dick, or Harry who wasn't at all your choice? Give me a break.

There was a lot of BS flying around an escort agency, I found. I never used to probe too deeply as I picked up on the fact that although happy, healthy(ish) women become escorts at this level, it obviously attracts women who shouldn't really be doing it; abused girls, abused in different ways, girls with self-esteem issues, issues with men and sex. But you never got the real story from them – it would be covered with bravado and too much makeup.

After I had escorted for a while, I came to believe that there should be a minimum age limit for doing the job – hard to be specific as everyone is different, but as a generalisation I would suggest mid-twenties maybe.

I saw eighteen or nineteen-year-olds come and go and it made me sad. This type of work shouldn't even cross a person of that age's mind; it's an option when a lot of other options have been exhausted. You also need some life experience to survive in it, know about people, men, sex, and just have had time to know yourself a bit, and no eighteen-year-old can say they have that behind them.

When I heard of an escort being badly treated or having any kind of negative incident it was, nine times out of ten, one of the younger girls. They weren't mature enough to read a situation, to judge the client, or indeed lay down the law and some clients can smell that a mile off, in fact, that's why they book the younger or new girls on the escorting scene, sadly.

Eventually though, after I had worked as an escort for a while, and as I have said, I just kept myself to myself. There were a lot of total idiots in escorting; it seemed to attract the sly and manipulative and an agency could get very bitchy and pathetic, which is not me at all.

There was, of course, a high staff turnover, as I'm sure you can imagine. One of the girls' tricks was, when a new girl joined the agency, especially if she was very pretty and sexy, to pretend to make friends with her – just chatting, but they would start to come out with their nightmarish escorting stories to put her off and get her to leave, whether they were true or not. Little cows! They did come and go regularly however for whatever reason, so I eventually just couldn't be bothered trying to get to know people – they wouldn't be there by next Tuesday!

I found the majority of escorts lived slightly to extremely chaotic lives. The word I always used was 'flakes', with some exceptions of course. There were plenty who had pretty good day jobs, well educated, as well as women who couldn't get or hold down a normal job if they tried. A lot were not business-like. I admire women who are entrepreneurial and work this business to their own advantage, the only way to do it I say. They all had their stories and good luck to them.

Steve, knowing how men's minds worked, would portray and 'sell' each escort as a type. When I started, he worked the phones, taking the bookings. The blonde bombshell, the Thai bride, the girl next door, the porn star, etc etc. With my dark looks he, in his wisdom, decided to change my temporary name of Katie and sell me as half-Italian. He changed my name to Gia, hmm, problemo! I had a few Italian-speaking clients, and as I knew approximately three words of Italian…well two, actually, I was caught out a few times and I told him to stop telling people I was the next Sophia Loren or I wouldn't shave my legs or pits anymore (well, that's a bit Italian, isn't it?). He duly obliged.

I was then given the name Gina and sold as the wild woman

as now that I had worked for a few months I was becoming known for accepting the weirder jobs and requests the agency got in! Like I told you in chapter one, I was no shrinking violet and not put off by all things weird, so any job Steve couldn't get other escorts to do, he would give to me. It didn't bother me; it was all the same old same old to me. From GFE, as I explained earlier, to gimp masks and rubber body bags (God knows where that particular client got that – Rubber Body Bags R Us, maybe?) It just made no odds; it was all just a job and a bit silly to me. In fact, the weirder jobs were often preferable, as there was less sex/touching and were more 'hands off'.

I liked a job where the client wanted to be tied up, for example, guaranteed no touchy, so me likey. That's why   I couldn't really understand why the other escorts would shy away from unusual jobs. I'd rather role-play as a gym mistress and count the clients' naked jumping jacks than do all that touchy-feely faff, bleugh!

Although domination-type jobs could be hard work mentally, especially if the client didn't know exactly what they wanted and left it to the escort to come up with all the details, scenarios and punishments. I'm not into all that stuff and I'm not a trained pro dominatrix, so it's hard to come up with ideas. I did have a domination client laugh at me when I was strutting around in all my latex clobber and being very mistress-like, and I ordered him to kneel before me and was considerate enough to put a cushion down for his poor knobbly knees! Not hardcore enough, apparently and I can definitely see his point.

I used to see one domination client who used to like being walked around on all fours with a dog lead around his neck. He supplied the lead, which was handy – but I had made him bark as we went walkies around the work flat and another escort who was in the kitchen at the time and didn't know the situation was apparently petrified and rang the office (or was it the RSPCA?) for advice. No need really, he was house-trained, so it was all good.

Pretty early on I used to see an Asian client who shall remain nameless. He just wanted his knob pulled and twisted for the whole appointment, and I mean PULLED AND TWISTED! He would complain if I wasn't pulling it hard enough, or indeed twisting. I was extremely shocked when in the last five minutes he got hard and came, I was so sure I'd have broken the bloody thing! Weirdly he always wanted to lie directly under the central light in the room we were using, even moving the bed to facilitate this little foible. I should have asked him about that one really. He had a fingernail fetish too, always wanted dark varnish, red or black, a common colour choice of the nail fetishist I find, and he wanted them dug into his ball sack, HARD.   I found doing dom work in the summer particularly uncomfortable. For these jobs there would often be an element of dress up in leather and rubber, and boy is all that stuff hard to get on and off in the sweaty summer heat. I got wedged into a rubber dress once and got all panicky and had to get the client to cut it off me with scissors. I was left a sweaty mess with hair like a bird's nest. Actually, I seem to remember he was the client who had a 'lick and stick' dildo he licked and erm... stuck on the wall and had asked me to back onto it, as it looked like a black veined rolling pin, I declined.

These clients I could understand paying for my services more than any other. I mean, whose partner was going to do that for free for a whole hour, for God's sake? Ball busting, as it's called is not too common a request, but common enough to warrant a mention.

I used to see one client quite regularly who liked me to take a running drop kick at his testicles. I would oblige, but boy, did I hold back. I have no desire to be up in court for GBH of a scrotum. You have to walk a fine line so as not to have to ring 999 at any point.

How the whole thing worked was thus: I would tell Steve what hours I wanted to work each week. When I was on shift, I would do my make-up and hair and make sure I was ninety-nine percent hair free, and that's a never-ending story in itself! Then just sit in my pyjamas, watching daytime television or generally pottering about. If I did venture out, I would never roam too far from home;

Steve wouldn't give us escorts a lot of time to get to the job usually. He was a tit like that – it wasn't him that was going to have to awkwardly make it up to the client for being late, and potentially be on the back foot, was it?

I found pretty early on that the work was constant if that's what you wanted, but the only times business would dip was school holidays – potential clients now had more childcare duties or they went on holiday with the family. In the run-up to payday, end of each month for obvious reasons. Another quiet time was when there was an important football match on, then how busy it got after depended on who had won, and I always found that Wednesdays were always a bit quieter work-wise, never worked that one out.

Once a client had chosen me from the website, he would ring Steve and book. Steve would then text me all the detail – the client's name, time and duration of the appointment, location, and any other details – like if the client wanted me to wear anything in particular. Most common being stockings and suspenders, of course. Or if they wanted water sports. For which, I would neck a couple of pints of water before I left the house in readiness.

Then the pyjamas would be stripped off and on would go the hold-up stockings and little black dress. One tip for prospective sex workers is this, do not wear anything for an escorting job that fastens up the back. Men can be cack-handed in such matters so relying on them to undo it for you is folly and you WILL want to get away swiftly after the appointment, not have some sausage-fingered client button you up all cock eyed. Honesty, the amount of shoe buckles I've had ruined by clients trying to undo them is unfathomable. Also, try not to wear anything that creases too easily, your clothes will end up strewn on the floor or hooked on something inadequate in the client's bedroom. I would always have my 'escort bag' packed (contents explained later!), so I'd grab that and head to the job in my car.

It could have been at one of the agency's three city centre flats or a venue chosen by the client, usually their house, hotel, and occasionally place of work. Not if they were a shelf stacker, you understand – not in aisle four. If I ever went to the workplace, it would be to see the boss after everyone had gone home for the night or at the weekend.

Once at the job and paid...actually, here is the most important rule, PAYMENT BEFORE ANY ITEM OF CLOTHING IS REMOVED! So, once paid, I would text Steve and let him know it was all going ahead. Same when I came out of the job, a text to let him know I was ok and done.

Sometimes a client would take a shine to me and want to 'extend', i.e., see me for longer than had been initially arranged. If so, I would text Steve to see if that was ok, to check he hadn't booked me in with another client straight after and so didn't have the time to spare. If I didn't like the client or just couldn't be bothered, I'd just tell him I was booked straight after anyway to get out of it.

One type of appointment I kept to a minimum was the overnighter, when a client booked you to stay, as the name suggests, overnight at his home or hotel. These overnighters can bring very good money, but God they drag on forever and a day (or night rather). Making fascinating conversation for an hour can be hard enough, but ALL NIGHT!!??!!

I mean, we escorts should be entitled to a decent amount of sleep, but the client would often take liberties and keep you up until all hours with annoying sex requests and weirdness at three AM. And when you did manage to get a few hours' sleep you slept with one eye open, like snoozing in a warzone or maybe when there was a prowler loose in your neighbourhood.

I had no interest in having an awkward bowl of cornflakes with some sheepish random person with less than delightful morning client breath, or worse when they tried to have morning sex to ring out every last penny...NO!

So that was the basics of how it all worked. As for my personal life, I was single, I wouldn't have chosen to escort if I had been with a partner. I would never do the job behind a partner's back, as many escorts in a relationship do. You are risking another person's sexual health for a start, which is a massive no-no in my eyes. It didn't seem to bother a lot of the other escorts – chasing the mighty dollar, I suppose.

However, I did keep it to myself to begin with in case I didn't stick with it, but once I had decided to keep doing it, I told all my friends. I didn't expect any of them to be outraged or have a negative reaction, I had good open-minded friends. I got a lot of questions, of course, and everyone wanted to know about any juicy or funny stories I had. I could go into gross detail with some, and they loved it and others I could tell just didn't really want to know – everyone is different regarding sexual matters, and I respected that. They totally understood why I was doing it but, other than that, weren't very interested after a while, they had their own things going on. I suppose I was lucky to not lose friends or come up against any resistance. A lot of escorts never tell another living soul, which I think must be a strain, it's a job you sometimes need to talk about, it's not all fun and games. It can be a very isolating job and lifestyle.

I didn't tell my family until years later. It's different for family and they just didn't need to know, they didn't need the worry, and when you live alone you can get up to pretty much anything and not a soul knows, phew!

CHAPTER 3

BECOMING A SEXPERT!

Well, there I was, dear reader, an escort. Gina. Not only that, but I was very successful; whenever I was on shift, I was in demand. Although I only worked occasionally, as I couldn't be bothered doing it too much, and financially didn't need to, the hourly rate was so high.

Something very practical and workaday here, but when you first begin to work as an escort, or indeed you have a few weeks or months break from it, you get all sorts of little health niggles: colds, sore throats, weird rashes, one after the other until your immune system toughens up after a few weeks and you are then invincible! Coming into intimate contact with so many people, I suppose.

Now this is quite personal to me, and I can't speak for all escorts, but I am very easily bored so that affected how I felt about this job too. Ok, that does not bode well for this book, but stick with me people. There is a lot of chatting in appointments, you see, and I don't find many people that interesting. Add into the mix that a lot of clients are literally shaking with nerves, affecting the quality of their patter to a massive extent and it results in one big yawn! That's one thing, but the client has also paid good money for you. You have to act as if they are fascinating, hilarious, and interesting, like a shitty date really! That, my friends, is EXHAUSTING! Recently, I was talking to a friend, and they presumed I just 'switched off' when I was with a client, especially during the sex. No, I never did. The client has paid for a service, they want good sex, good company.

Read on and I will complain about clients and the job itself but at the end of the day, I wouldn't have done it if I couldn't have done it well.

The actual sex is the least of the job for me, (although most civilians obsess over that bit) at least once you are doing that you can just crack on, the cash is in your purse, happy days. It's the "geisha"- like bit that's the problem. Most escorts in my experience agree. I think the perception may be that clients shag n go, not true, most ring every last penny out of their time. I once had a client who talked for half of a two-hour appointment about the industry he was in, - the car tyre industry...nonstop, bit like a tyre going down a hill in fact, haha. I was almost cock eyed with boredom, but the award-winning actress in me was FASCINATED.

A lot of escorts I talked to over the years all wished all clients would just fuck them and go, it's all the boring 'o, so where do you work?' crap that is the problem. Once I had left the agency and was an independent escort taking my own bookings the problem was the booking process. So many clients made what should have been a simple process, so hard, such a performance. To the point that I would wonder if we were actually speaking the same language, it was like wrangling toddlers, bizarre. This, for me, was the hardest part of the job, without exception.

One regular client I had was obsessed with the American wrestling scene and to minimise sexual activity, on his less-than-fresh duvet cover, I used to wrack my brain for questions about these boring characters from this silly world of wrestling. By the end I knew more than him, I think! As every escort knows if you keep 'em talking there's less sex, the holy grail!

I was getting a lot more experienced though and had ditched the kimono! Generally, escorts live in hold-up stockings, in my experience. They give men that stockings look most of them like without the utter impracticality of a suspender belt. They are complimentary if your legs have 'issues', cellulite, dumpiness or they have the look of corned beef. I personally always wore little sports socks under them for comfort and warmth in winter. The stockings were 60 deniers so you couldn't see them, I'm not daft.

What a palaver I had finding the perfect hold-ups though, God they are hard to get right if you have any amount of fat at the tops of your legs! Again, ASDA wins out here, I'm sure all their hold-up stocking sales are to escorts…and possibly bank robbers.

Actually, that reminds me of a client who enjoyed 'encasement'. He liked to put one of my stockings over his head and assume the look of a comedic, sexually frantic bank robber during the whole process, hmm that stocking was unwearable after that, just kept falling down. In fact, I'm sure whenever I put on a pair of hold-ups, I go into a kind of robot escort persona, a little 'Pavlov's dog'.

Now, I mentioned earlier that an escort has an 'escort bag'. This is her whole life when she is working. Usually, a fairly big bag with various pockets, practical yet fairly stylish, although I have known escorts to carry teeny tiny little bags and pull all things escort out of them like Mary Poppins magical sack! No idea how they did that. These escort bags have a few basics: Condoms, three different sizes, from the euphemistically named 'comfort fit' (small) to the rather grandiose 'king size' (self-explanatory). Note: never let your 'comfort fit' client see you open a comfort fit condom packet – open it in your escort bag and deposit the wrapper in said bag, quick!

Personally, I eschew all, what I call, comedy condoms: ribbed, coloured, flavoured, because when I have used them with clients, I always feel like the client will think I'm taking the Mickey, nobody wants a green polka dot erection, after all. I did at one point think of designing an 'escort tool belt' for the busy jobbing hooker. Having all the essentials around your waist, within easy reach would be a blessing during an appointment. Same as a traditional tool belt but each compartment is designed to fit more escort-friendly items, lube compartment, condom compartment, dildo holster, maybe in a choice of feminine/fun fabrics…wipe clean.

Next was baby wipes. All hail the baby wipe! As an escort, you live or die by your baby wipes. The obvious use is after sex to clean yourself up between your legs, but believe you me, sometimes clients must be cleaned, like cleaning a baby after removing a nappy. It never fails to amaze me, a booking with an escort is not a spontaneous shag – the client always has time for a shower, yet in a bizarre move, some don't have one, hence the escort having to clean under a fetid foreskin. I honestly think they think we won't notice, or they just have so little respect for prostitutes and/or themselves they think we won't mind, but… we do mind. The circumcised penis is a sex workers God send! Sweaty, clammy balls with the wide and varied associated smells, are not.

When I first started, I would feel awkward about getting my wipes out to clean my client like I'm his carer, but I soon became immune to awkwardness and would just do it in a very practical way. Hey, why should I feel awkward, you're the one offering up a dirty member for my consideration, (sometimes the smeg had turned brown it was that old) for God's sake. Of course, it's preferable to ask them to take a shower if there's one at hand, it takes up five or ten minutes of the appointment, which is great.

Rule two after getting the money upfront. DO NOT MAKE PRESUMTIONS RE SMEGMA. Do not be fooled by a nice suit, clean fingernails, or any form of male grooming in fact. Any foreskin is capable of being packed with the stuff once drawn back. You don't make that mistake twice I can tell you…looks can be deceptive where smeg is concerned.

On one job I ended up with a tiny bit of what we shall euphemistically call 'matter' in my mouth before I let slip my escort façade and said 'urgh' and dropped his cock like a hot stone……. I could not believe my lack of foreskin vigilance after ten years in the job!

Baby wipes were also used to 'have a bath' as I would phrase it. If Steve had booked an escort for two appointments back-to-back and a shower wasn't available, the escort basically had to go over her whole body with wipes, getting rid of the smell of the last client and mimic the smell of the freshly showered individual. I personally would use one to have a sweep (which I attractively christened, a scrape….) of my innards whilst sitting in my car (having scanned my surroundings well for inquisitive passers-bye) immediately before I went to knock on the client's door if I had very recently come off my period and may still be ever so slightly bloody. I thought I was the only sex worker at the agency to do this, but I found out others did it too, there is literally no glamour in this job.

Wipes were also very helpful if a client had cum on your clothing/shoes/hair. Nobody wants to walk down the road splattered with jizz – fact. Some escorts I knew would carry a wig in their kit bag, to provide anonymity. Hmm, would have thought you would have stood out a mile in an ill-fitting haystack wig which I found they generally were and, note to wig wearers, we can all still see your face so, unless you choose to wear your glorious crown topper back to front, everyone still knows who you are. Apart from the fact that a wig ain't gonna stay on your bonce long during sex, therefore, I conclude, it was all a bit pointless. I did have a client for donkey's years who, all of a sudden after seeing him for about 6 years, asked me to wear wigs during our bookings. He provided a long blonde thing that once squeezed over my massive head plus my thick hair combo, gave me the appearance of a young Rick Parfitt from the rock band Status Quo.

Other items in the escort bag were a sex toy, most sex workers opt for a vibrator as you can pop a condom over it for multi-partner usage and it's the easiest sex toy to rinse.

Lubricant, (for anything anal mainly but some clients are so unattractive, or they bang away for so bloody long (is there anything more tedious?) they can actually dry up your vagina, so it's a must-have) make-up and toiletries in general, especially perfume; sex smells, let's be honest.

When I am with a client, I often wonder if sexually this is how they are with their wives and girlfriends. In my estimation maybe 80% of clients are in a relationship, a lot admit it, some don't. Sometimes I turn up to a client's house and they will totally deny they have a partner. Hmmm, who do all the women's clothes and toiletries belong to then? Oh, and by the way, single men never have ornamental cuddly toys on the marital bed. I never know why they bother to lie, the guilt I suppose, but escorts don't care, it's them that's cheating, not us.

As an independent escort, meaning I take my own bookings as opposed to them being taken through an agency, a lot of clients inform you they are married when they try to book and ask if I mind?! Why would I? In fact, a lot of clients go into a lot of detail about their looks, age, level of fitness (?), how clean they are (hmm sexy), and many other very uninteresting personal facts as if it makes a difference to ME! Mate, be the ugliest, most unfit man on earth, be 4 foot 3, smell of onions, I don't care, get your wallet out, job done.

As an escort I get a fair few men contact me as if they have found me on an actual dating site, so much so that I have to eventually ask them if they know I am a sex worker and expected payment? They always say they do, which makes their approach even more moronic and deluded. Most would react as if I am being a bit base or vulgar to raise the subject of coin and definitely as if I should be flattered (so flattered as a mere slut that I will bestow free sex on him possibly). Now I can imagine a few of you readers thinking that these are nice considerate things to do but they aren't really. Ok, they aren't cruel or hurtful (time-wasting, yes) but they are to do with the rampant male ego, don't kid yourself.

A huge proportion of prospective clients would make such a song and dance of it all, sending a million e-mails and texts, flapping about when booking me really was a simple thing. I got it, they were new to it all and nervous but what has that got to do with me? I did not have the inclination to reply to 200 texts asking the same question in 200 different ways and no matter how much I hinted at them to stop texting, they alas, would not. Don't think a lot of men take hints too well. Although when I ended up having to be blunt with them, I, of course was being totally insensitive and harsh. Maybe they had me confused with their therapist or grandmother? (I would make a brilliant sex therapist by the way).

I regularly felt very sorry for the partners of many clients if what they were doing with me was what they had to endure for free! I would always try to get out of kissing, but sometimes it was unavoidable. Now I have kissed men and women and I have never kissed a woman that was terrible at it, but by heck have I kissed a lot of clients who are beyond terrible. It is my theory that many men think their tongue while kissing, is an extension of their cock.   They just make it as big and stiff as possible and stick it in your mouth. Someone please tell me what I'm supposed to DO with that? Suck it, bite it, hang my washing on it? The mouth also seems to be permanently open, again, WHY? Don't get me started on man breath. I will admit I have known a couple of women with stale breath, but some men take the biscuit. Actually, though a man's bad breath can often invade a blow job! You may already know what I'm driving at here, if not it's the fact that as one gives oral sex to a dog-breathed man he naturally can start breathing heavily and as he is usually looking at the action his breath is directed at the top of one's head/facial/and more importantly, nasal area…. phew! Sometimes there is just no escape! I actually christened that phenomenon 'blow job breath', which could mean something else too, now I think about it.

This is when I would pity the wives and girlfriends, they had to live with these things day in day out…wow! As for the sex these women must have to tolerate, now maybe they themselves are a bit crap in bed too or just don't have much experience or let's hope, just aren't that bothered, but how do you put up with Mr. Damp hands or Mr au naturale pubes, disgusting! (TIP; - wipe off lip gloss before sucking a long pubed ball sack or you WILL regret it) or Mr. Lie-On-Top-Of-Me-So-Heavy-I-Can't-Breath-And-I-Feel-Like-A-Bag-Of-Cement-Has-Fallen-From-A-Great-Height-On-To-My-Torso? Or awkwardness of all awkwardness, Mr. No-Rhythm. My darling pick a rhythm and stick to it. As the woman during sex, trying to force a rhythm-free man into a steady rhythm in most sexual positions is bloody hard! Makes me a bit angry, I mean, I'm doing literally everything here mate, help me out a bit! I will only try for so long then just give up and turn 'rag doll' and simply bide my time. Only so much I can do! My theory is that a lot of men have sex at 60, the way they were doing it at 16. They simply will not be told!

The men that stand out are 'the silent ones', we shall call them. I would be having sex with them, and they would just lie there like a corpse, or if they were behind me their hands would be limp around my waist and totally and completely silent. Like it was a boring obligation; with no concept that they could be enjoying themselves. No passion, no excitement, no nothing really. I imagine this is how some couples would act while in the middle of an ad break during 'Emmerdale'. Thing is, why book an escort for that kind of sex, what's the point? And they would often book again, so it clearly wasn't anything I was doing wrong, if that's what you are thinking, you tinkers. I was always quite surprised when it dawned on me a lot of men had never played with their own nipples. When asked by my good self if they liked their nips played with or sucked, they had no idea!? Why would you not have touched your own nipples for God's sake men? A lot of you certainly are never shy to touch your dicks as you are walking down the street! Another thing I find weird is how some men don't seem sure if they have cum occasionally……. how can you not know? Then again, I believe women's orgasms are more intense and are therefore impossible to miss!

I had experienced a pretty varied sex life before escorting, but nobody sees as much variety as an escort. In my private life, I had honestly never had bad sex. I'd had pointless sex, and not great sex, but not BAAAD. Until I escorted!

One client once licked the tops of my thighs for absolutely ages. I was confused, but he seemed very into it, so I pretended it was having some kind of effect and wasn't pointless or odd. It's not part of the job to criticise anyone's performance – it's frowned upon by clients, don't you know? I thought it could be his way of building himself up to actually going anywhere near my clit but, nah, he just kept on keeping on. It dawned on me that he thought this WAS oral sex. How quaint. So, I dutifully put him out of his misery and gave him the old fake orgasm and he looked very proud of himself. Had no previous partner ever questioned this technique, such as it was?

Over the years we all had clients that would do something very odd like that, obviously thinking it was an acceptable and normal sexual practice. In all such cases it is advisable to join in the pretence, do NOT question or criticise them. Hey, what harm does it do? In fact, knowing how to time your fake orgasm as an escort is vital. Once you can tell the client is doing the activity, he believes will make you cum, time it from there. Do not pretend to cum too soon, that's beyond fake and the client may be dubious, but stretch things out to kill some time. Like comedy, timing is everything. I do however occasionally, have to put 'the emergency' orgasm into practice. This is a fake orgasm that does not observe the usual timing rules because whatever the client is doing to try to make me cum is so sick wrenching as to be counterproductive, i.e. I will spew up and spoil the atmosphere. This practice whilst vital in your repertoire is not to be abused.

If I was working in one of the agency's flats and I knew another escort was knocking about in there, I'd do a comedy orgasm, stick a bit of opera in or maybe farmyard noises. Once the client had gone, we would have a chuckle about it. I know most escorts have had clients declare 'I love you' at the point of climax which is at once funny for the escort and presumably embarrassing for the client.

One escort I knew had a regular who would shout 'I'm arriving' as he climaxed.

Now, as most escorts would agree, the best clients are just clean, polite, and quick. Speaking of which, I think my speediest client was a man who worked on the oil rigs off Scotland. He had booked an hour's appointment and he came to one of the flats but as soon as I had opened the door to him he got a text – he was 'on call' for his job and had to get to the airport to fly out to a rig within a couple of hours, so looking down at my ample bosoms and now in a dilemma – boobies versus work – he asked if he could play with my boobs (fully clothed boobies, everyone) for a minute for the full fee. Well, that my friend, is what you call a no-brainer.

The jobs I found a welcome change were a 'two-girl' booking, when a client books two escorts together for a threesome. Not for any deeply erotic reasons, as you may have gathered by now readers, but because they are half the work. There's another escort there to share the burden of sexual activity and conversation with a client full of nervous excitement, and the fact that they are usually just so very happy that two women have their boobies out in front of them, it's half the job done right there.

I was the official inventor of 'boob wars', the general idea being we two escorts would kneel on the bed close up face to face and proceed to whack our tits against the other woman's tits, inducing open-mouthed agog expressions from the client, along with a semi-erect penis. Just something to fill two minutes of the appointment, added value, I liked to see it as and yes, I always won boob wars…my boobs are bloody huge.

I had had sex with one woman before becoming an escort, so I wasn't a total newbie to the wonders of the female body. It wasn't a big deal to be with another escort on a job. I know a lot of the other escorts, mainly straight women (I only knew of a couple of lesbians working), would cringe at doing two-girl jobs to start with. But once they saw how much work there was doing it alone and had got used to the job a bit more, they started to offer the service as well.

Two-girl jobs could be a right laugh anyway. I am a born show-off and quite creative and would come up with roleplay scenarios. I remember on one job I suggested to the client that I and the other escort acted out a gang initiation ceremony, where at one point I was whipping her arse with her knickers. We were all in kinks – it can be a fun job for sure, if the alternative is sitting in a works canteen reading signs about next week's super fun/ mega pointless dress down Friday wondering who has farted and how long you can get away with hiding in the toilets during your shift for next to no money.

I never understood why escorts didn't want to do two-girl jobs initially, I mean you are going to be having sex with men who will turn your stomach and who you wouldn't fancy in a million years, so why was it so hard to do the same with a woman. It's all just pretending and acting, so what difference did it make and at least it's one less cock to have to look at. Made a pleasant change, I thought.

By the same token, some escorts wouldn't see Asian or black men, again, what bloody difference does it make? It's not a blind date, you buffoons! Before the client for the two-girl job arrived, I would have a chat with the other escort and divvy up the work; I'd always ask if she would do all the kissy-touchy stuff, and I'd do anything weird he wanted. They were always quite happy with this arrangement.

The other type of appointment I appreciated was the two male client three-some or MMF, as it is known as in the trade. The thing with these jobs is I would fi

CHAPTER 4

LET'S BE PRACTICAL

I think I'm right in saying, especially when it comes to sex, women are generally one hell of a lot more practical, probably due to our keeping our brains switched on throughout proceedings. And our lower use of pornography, which often depicts the most ridiculously impractical sex ever and makes a lot of men think such ridiculousness is possible. If women in general are sexually more practical, then the female escort is the ultimate. After all, we have a job to do and there are a lot of implications to this.

Firstly, I must get this off my chest, a lot of clients request/ expect appointments at all hours of the day and night, maybe like escorts are nocturnal or have nothing else to do, like a day job, family, friends, a social life, the need to sleep and eat. Many clients genuinely seem surprised that we have other things to do and aren't just sitting and waiting to have sex with them at 3am!

I also think many believe we have some kind of super-duper escort transportation device, as very often they want us at their house 15 miles away in 10 minutes…in rush hour…in a blizzard, like we have a futuristic jet pack maybe? We don't. Quite a few clients also make a habit of texting me furiously when they KNOW I must be driving to our appointment, thing is I need to keep pulling over and checking the texts in case they are cancelling or some other hot news.

When we do turn up, many clients, maybe first-timers who book an escort to go to their homes, seem to think we are going to turn up looking like some pantomime hooker (I don't recall the pantomime that features a hooker, but you get my gist), which they are petrified of (nosey neighbours) all PVC bra and thigh boots. Firstly, it's usually freezing in this country, so there's that, PVC bras don't keep in the heat, but we also don't really want to stick out a mile ourselves, looking beyond stupid. Yes, I have seen some escorts turn up for appointments looking like a character from a 1993 episode of The Bill, an episode about a poor old brass who'd got herself in trouble with some brute maybe and owns a terrible house coat, but they were usually from shabbier agencies, the ones where the girl's profile pictures featured their tumble dryer in the background, for example.

Most importantly, we are on the clock, I would always wear a tight-fitting watch, so it didn't swivel on the wrist and I'd make sure the face was positioned where I could see it at a glance, whatever position I found myself in! It sat on the same wrist as my 'blow job bobble', the hair bobble I – and I found out soon enough – most escorts with hair longer than chin length wear one on their wrist for jobs in readiness. I would quickly tie my hair back with it when a BJ was on the cards, as many of you will know long hair gets stuck in your lip gloss and wraps itself around the cock shaft during cock sucking so you just end up sucking on your own hair mainly.

I liked to wear my hair down for jobs, glamorous, yes but practical, no. Clients can be very clumsy and just love to lie on your hair, rendering you immobile and depositing spit and spunk into it or just generally pulling it about in a very annoying 'I'm so passionate' way and ruining your 'do'. Same reason I would generally decline 'let's have sex in the shower' appointments, and the added fact I could never be sure how clean their bathroom was going to be! I probably had another client to see or had to go to the supermarket or something straight after, I don't need to look like Ken Dodd or a drowned rat whilst doing so– thanks, fella!

Another phenomenon was having my foundation licked off! I had never experienced this strange practice until I became an escort, and I mean just as I say, licking my face like a human makeup remover. Lots of the escorts had it happen, it's a 'thing'.

I soon put a stop to that, my foundation was not cheap! I would have had somewhere to go after, with half a face of make-up left, erm, no way! And which lunatic invented the romantically named 'spitty blow job' please?? Spending half of an appointment drowning in my own spittle, nose to belly button, is not only gross, but it is another practice that has a detrimental effect on one's makeup. It leaves you a bit dehydrated too.   Having big boobs, tit wanks were often requested. Giving a tit wank is one of the most ridiculous things a woman can find herself doing in my humble opinion, they look stupid from the giver's point of view, are hard physical work, and sometimes give you the feeling of having your tits ripped off. I never know where to look when I'm giving one either. I always carried foundation in my kit bag though after that…just in case. Suppose I should have had a bottle of Lucozade in there too to rehydrate, but I didn't. I mean, I'm not easily grossed out or prissy, my motto was always 'whatever substance you get on you can always be washed off, so chill out'.

Saying that, I recall letting a client give me a facial, i.e., cumming on my face, as I was heading back home after this particular job and didn't mind having traces of crusty spunk on my face and adorning my hair so let him take aim approximately at my nose. Well, he came on my cheek, and it was the consistency of cottage cheese with a slight green tinge. I know this because it was so stubborn it didn't drop off as I arose from the sofa, and I looked at it in the mirror over his fireplace. Was it the green tinge that made it smell so? I don't know, but it didn't help that it was an inch from my left nostril. I rediscovered a gag reflex I thought I had lost and flicked it into the fire. At least he didn't come in my eye which some, mostly younger clients are prone to do if they have an impressively far-ranging ejaculation that the escort just can't dodge. Leading to a bloodshot eyeball. I called this cumjunctivitis.   Although this is preferable to some spunk getting lodged up your nasal canal when the client has cum unexpectedly and I hadn't had time to close my throat off in time.

It then remerges into your throat an hour later stinking to high heaven. Truly one of the worst things to happen to a person since time began, especially if one is driving. It's dangerous.

As I mentioned before, baby wipes are an escort's best friend, the ultimate practicality, cleaning fetid knobs, and you may find it surprising how many men expect a good rimming with a crusty old A hole, offering the thing up for my delectation. I mean there's no dignity in that, is there people? Although I've had a few clients who, as fans of being rimmed, have gone at their arse hole with a scrubbing brush and disinfectant, I think, and it's been much appreciated. My one hot tip whilst rimming a fellow is to never let the horror film 'The Human Centipede' enter your thoughts. I did have a client recently ask as he bent over, arse in my face, if I could rim him and suck him off at the same time? I told him he was being silly, and he could see I only had one mouth! I tromboned him to oblivion, he gave me a box of chocolates after.

I once visited a client who had only just returned home after a three-day stag weekend in Blackpool. When I pulled his foreskin back, I simply had never seen anything like it, except maybe on an episode of the TV show, 'Embarrassing Bodies'. So much smegma and he just lay there, didn't give a care, he was all Blackpooled out, I think, but I went through three baby wipes getting rid of all that and then sent him to the shower. A little tip to any new escorts out there; - spray the backs of your hands with strong perfume if your clients' dick/balls smell dodgy, in this way if you hold the base of his cock as you suck you can only smell your own hand, simples!

We escorts would all clean ourselves down with baby wipes at every opportunity. Wipes are good for cleaning a used dildo or dong adding a nice fresh smell. I should use them to wipe down clients' armpits too as some men have no shame just lying back, arms behind their heads, and gassing me with the delightful oniony aroma of their pits. Like chemical warfare really. I used to let the acrid pit slide most of the time, in escorting you have to pick your battles, pick the lesser of two evils, you see? If they were 'acceptably un-fresh' I would just go with it as I may have to put my foot down about some ridiculous sex thing they wanted to do later on. Probably something tiresome from a porn film, or that was going to ruin my make-up…again.

Porn: Why do the people in porn always look so angry and serious? I find it usually looks joyless, sex with all the individuality and human connection stripped. Also, don't most people crack a smile or something close to it when they shag, not look like they've got a parking ticket? I mean, yes, ok, life may have taken a few awful sad turns for the actors to end up in a porno, but the director really should be telling them to smile. Remember you're in showbiz, darling!

Don't get me started on why so much porn often depicts grown women made up to look much younger, long socks, pigtails. Or are depicted as looking distressed, weepy, or like they are in blatant agony. Recently I have noticed a trend in porn where the woman involved looks unaware that she is being filmed, in other words, this isn't porn it is abuse.

The vocabulary used to describe scenes, brutal, ruin, slag, slut. Makes me so angry and physically sick. Why men who have the need (and who are probably woefully inadequate) to brutalise a woman to get off, have their pathetic needs catered for is sickening. I am not an expert in the field and generally only see porn if a client is watching it when I am with them at home or the short porno clips independent escorts sell on their online profiles to advertise their services, some of which I am presuming has been conceived by some man or other and not the actual escort herself (unless she has not an ounce of self-respect). Videos such as the escort engaging in various sex acts with the word 'slut' written on her forehead or giving a blow job while the BJ recipient spat on her. This side of sex work makes me angry and has nothing to do with how I conduct myself. The sad thing is these sex workers are probably making a fortune, many men love that kind of thing. I'd rather starve than serve up that shit. As an escort, I would get offers of porn work quite regularly.

To be honest, the only time I would consider the offers was when I was at a low in my life, feeling lost sad, and desperate. I do however make short explicit videos for my online profile as most independent escorts do. I feel more comfortable with these films as I have absolute control over the content and context. A few of them still make me cringe, it was never my dream to film myself 'fingering both holes' (which is one of my best sellers) and put it online, but they are a great money maker and advert for my more expensive services. My videos are never degrading or 'wrong' in any way.

I am not particularly interested in watching porn and I have heard too many unhappy backstories of the people in it as well as exploitative practices within the industry that makes me uncomfortable, what exactly am I watching? No idea, and that's the problem. I don't feel like wanking off to someone's sadness and desperation. Hey, I am not an expert, I am sure there will be porn actors about to rip up this book, swearing they are happy doing what they are doing, but I am not clueless either and I just don't feel comfortable watching it. Anyway, where is the porn reflecting a straight woman's view of sex, please, we are equally involved in the act, and we are not men.

Porn can be the bane of the escort's life, and a weird blessing – how many times had a client got his phone out and shown me a clip from a porno involving something back-breaking for me to perform? On the other hand, it can also be a relief if a client knows exactly what he wants, it takes the pressure off me to come up with stuff. I mean do you know how hard it is to be inventive sexually with some man who's just wandered in off the street, dressed like an 80s dad. It is almost painful to have to wrack one's brain so much.

Anyway, the porno things they want to act out are generally completely undoable. The actress in the film has probably had to endure hours of physio between takes because of the outlandish and deeply unattractive position she has been forced into, gurning away like a lunatic. Maybe she's had surgery to widen all orifices, but either way, it's not happening, dude, put the phone away and I'll tell you what IS going to happen.

That's how I would always play it unless it was something bog standard that weirdly enough, they seemed to think was exotic. Like the client who took half of his appointment building up the courage to tell me he wanted a blow job where he was standing up and I was kneeling…erm, ok my friend, you absolute pervert!

That reminds me of a lot of clients who ask for very basic things, like a blow job, or sex with me on top, and are gobsmacked when I just agree, no bother. It will then transpire that 'the missus', who was their only ever sexual partner, never let them do anything but turn the light off and pull up her nighty. So, to them anything is outrageous. Very easy clients, those ones, I must say.

Some clients get carried away somewhat though, like the clients who want to extend the appointment; they will ask to do this early on when they are all over-excited and raging. I usually say, 'Well, let's just wait until you have cum, then we will see'. Without fail, once they have it out of their system, they change their minds and look a bit sheepish.

Another thing that is sometimes asked for, not often but enough to warrant a mention, is when they are randy as hell and want to swallow their own spunk. I am to spit it into their mouths after oral sex. I only ever knew one client to actually do it and to be honest he looked like he was going to hurl it straight back up, and who can blame the poor bugger? As I'm sure anyone who regularly takes spunk in the mouth, there is a little area in there where the man cums, (as an escort with time-honed skills, you can actually smell the spunk before it ever emerges, as well as feel it gurgling up from the balls if you have your hand in the right place on the shaft) you can direct the excretion so it cannot be tasted, the flavour of jizz being an acquired taste. RULE NUMBER THREE; DO NOT LOOK AT THE SPUNK AFTER YOU WADDLE TO THE BATHROOM AND SPIT IT OUT. THERE ARE SO MANY WEIRD AND WONDERFUL VARIETIES THAT I FOR ONE DO NOT WANT TO KNOW WHICH ONE I HAVE IN MY GOB AT ANY GIVEN TIME. CLOSE THINE EYES, SPIT, RINSE AWAY, OPEN THINE EYES.

Lots of men wanted a finger or vibrator up their bum but would always precis the whole thing with 'I'm not gay'. I wouldn't even dignify that with a response, just shove my finger up… wrapped in a condom and lube, before you ask. I personally would be very gentle on insertion, considerate you know... unlike most men! Quite a few men ask for their cock to be bitten really hard during oral or to feel my teeth scaping up and down the shaft, I can't imagine I'd like that if I had a penis and personally if I feel teeth during oral I find a quick, light, crack on the back of the head sorts it. Now...WHAT IS IT WITH MEN AND FRANTIC VAGINAL FINGERING???! Who has been encouraging this?

I believe there is an argument for teaching boys, during school sex education, that vaginas are not made of vulcanised rubber, and most can't take a man's big fat fingers being rammed in so fast and furiously it rattles the woman's fillings!

Also, men, what do some of you think you are going to find with all the digging around you do up there? You do realise it's not a bottomless pit, don't you? Saying that I do sometimes get clients up who seem to just want to look 'up' my vagina. Quite often youthful Asian students, in the country to study, presumably other things besides my plumbing? They would gaze up there, seemingly bemused. I wonder if they were waiting for something to pop out and hit them on the nose?! If I had a pound for every time I have told a client to stop trying to pick my nose via my vagina I would have circa £1,235. Men: - vaginas are delicate, massively sensitive things. STOP BELIEVING/ RENACTING PORN...NOW!

I think another thing porn has done, is make men want anal sex more like it's not sometimes massively painful with the risk of an anal prolapse thrown in! However, I did use to offer it, but some days for no reason it just was not possible, not even with someone with a cock like a betting shop pen and that was that. Quite a few men have erections that bend markedly to one side or point down a bit and weirdly they would seem quite confused when I refused them anal sex for that reason. Ouch! I mean, have they never seen how bent their cock is or what? Often a client would ask "have you cum?" after about 30 seconds of anal sex! Sorry?

Are you aware of where the clitoris is to be found? A little clue, nowhere near the arse hole, and by the way no woman cums after 30 seconds of ANYTHING. The thing is my pretend sex noises are just too damn believable, but 30 seconds!? I took anal sex (A- Levels) in sex work speak, off the menu due to an incident where I bled a little after the act, it scared me, and I decided not to offer it anymore. Rather sickeningly many clients who had been offered anal sex in the past, often tried to persuade me to do it again once I had stopped doing it and knew the reason why, no other way to put it than, selfish cunts!

What would annoy me though was a lot of clients wouldn't pluck up the courage to approach the subject until the last five minutes of their appointment! Well anal sex takes easing into, and a lot of deep breaths, so they should have spoken up half an hour ago, silly Billies, and by the way boys, when a woman tells you anal sex hurts sometimes, believe her, it does. Porn stars presumably spend hours sitting on butt plugs to stretch them, the average woman does not, she really does have better things to do, and DO NOT just shove a surprise and more importantly un-lubed digit up anyone's arse during sex – it's extremely irritating and bloody painful and I'd like to slap anyone who does it…and so would a few of my non-escort friends, by the way. Yes, boys, we do talk!

I can tell a client who watches a lot of porn, and I'm referring to the type of porn straight men generally watch, which in my view is usually just a manual for bad sex (bad sex for women anyway) with few exceptions, within about three seconds of proceedings. It's mostly the under forties I'd say, and I am aware that ninety-nine percent of men of all ages watch porn, but generally, older men have experience of real sex and real women too and understand porn isn't real.

But there are a lot of men whose main sexual experience is porn and that's apparent in their technique and attitude, it's obvious and quite sad. In fact, I find it's some of the older, average-looking, unassuming clients that are the best in bed. They have often disclosed that they usually have had only a handful of partners, but ones they have cared for, had meaningful relationships with, and therefore have actually taken the time to attune themselves to each woman's need. They care about their partner's experience and are mature. If a client was to make me cum it would generally be one of these types of men. Now when I first came with a client, I stressed about it so much, he was an older man, in his 60's probably and I beat myself up about it; - How could this happen?! What does that make ME? It took me a long time to just accept that some men are just good at what they do, and it was just a mechanical response to that, I'm only human, I have nerve endings for God's sake. The job is hard enough without beating yourself up about having an orgasm.

Eventually, after I had worked for the agency for a while and was one of the more experienced women, a few of the other escorts would have the same concern and I would tell them what I have just told you, basically life is too short to stress about it. When it happens to me it is never because I find the client attractive it's simply a basic physical response, hey, if someone is good they are good, physically unattractive or not although if I found myself in danger of cumming with someone I really didn't feel comfortable with for any reason I would deploy the 'emergency orgasm' and bailout.

Often 'jack the lad' types aren't always that great, again I'm presuming they have relied on their looks and had zillions of partners they haven't necessarily cared about, so haven't learned a thing. Fatter men and men with smaller cocks tend to pride themselves on their oral prowess and would insist on displaying their skills first. Not always the case, but just my observations.

The looks of confusion and disappointment on some men's faces when I had to explain why the porn scene, they wanted to act out wasn't practical or when the sex we were having wasn't going down exactly like the film was – just pathetic really. I mean real sex involves not being a twelve-year-old double-jointed gymnast, stopping to put a condom on or lube up, fanny around looking for a pillow to put under one's knees or yank your hair from under them or actually breathe through your mouth; a lot of men seem to think women can breathe through their ears. In summary, as I'm sure you will agree, real sex can be clumsy, stoppy-starty, uncomfortable, and just is what it is…practical stuff. Oh, yes and I have to be able to check my watch at all times, of course.

Us escorts would get the brunt of the porn fascination. It seems a lot of men even in this day and age don't feel they can ask their partners to perform things they have seen in porn or indulge their fantasies, but they feel able to ask an escort. Granted, some of the things they wanted to do were just gross and would, I can imagine, render them deeply unattractive to their partners, so maybe it was for the best. I mean who wants to spend hours massaging a prostate for free for God's sake.

One irritating but thought-provoking incident inspired by the overuse of porn went like this. I had been booked by a young lad. He said he was nineteen – this was when I first started escorting as later on, I raised my age limit to twenty-five and over. It just got too 'icky' for want of a better word to see clients any younger than that.

As I looked younger than I was, Steve had me on the website as eight years younger and nobody ever batted an eyelid and I used to wonder if these lads would freak out if they knew my real age. They thought I was an 'older woman' believing I was maybe thirty when in reality I was knocking on forty. Setting this rule did do away with quite a few bookings I used to get from young lads booking an older escort to act out a fantasy they had about one of their mother's friends. I also remember turning down one young man who wanted us to be having sex whilst he was on the phone with his aunty, I don't like the idea of people not knowing they are involved in something, it's disrespectful. Maybe his aunty would have found it hilarious if she had known but I did not know that so I would rather not do it.

Anyway, I got to this young client's flat, which is typical lone man style looked like he had just moved in the previous day – no décor to speak of, unpacked boxes of belongings all over the place, so I was surprised when I found out he had lived there about six months!

He was watching porn when I arrived, which is fairly common with clients, but he seemed distracted. I asked if anything was wrong and he asked my name, which I had already given, and he continued to look confused. I worked out fairly quickly that he had booked the wrong escort and didn't know how to say it. I asked if this was the case, and he proceeded to show me the two profiles he had been trying to choose between, one was indeed mine and the other was another similar-looking escort. He had accidentally, it seemed, booked me and then went on to make no secret of his disappointment. Charmed I'm sure, thought I.

He forced himself to make do with me and we sat watching this porn, in which the actress featured was dark-haired, big-boobed just like me and the other escort he actually preferred. The only difference being, the actress was very 'porny', with fake boobs, hair, nails, pout, overacting to within an inch of her awful ankle-breaking shoes. Well, this lad continued to look put out and was a bit stroppy in a monosyllabic way as we proceeded to the bedroom.

We got undressed and his disappointment did not diminish. I asked, 'What's wrong?' in a semi-considerate way. My actual thoughts were, 'You are a tedious little bastard, aren't you?' He then piped up 'I wish you were sexier' and proceeded to look over my body as if I had the lurgy. Mmm, I wish I'd gone to university, mate, but I didn't. I'm here with the most charmless man alive, but hey, that's life. The first thing I said was, 'You're not getting any money back, it's your fault you booked the wrong escort.' You've got to get the basics sorted first in this job, reader.

I knew what he meant by 'sexier' – more 'porny', fake, flawless, not a spot, not a stretch mark, not an ounce of cellulite. Well, I have all three because I'm an actual real woman, a human being. This is what women look like, we wobble! He didn't know that though – he had only ever watched porn. He was a virgin. I honestly can't remember what the outcome of that situation was, it was many years ago, but I wish I squirted my lube up his nose… both holes.

His communication with me from the minute I walked in was as if I were unfeeling – an object. Now I did not take the remark personally, as he was a bewildered fool, who I didn't know from Adam, but he had been conditioned by porn, no experience of real girls, real life, just porn, and that makes me quite angry.

I often get clients telling me "Be really dirty for me", whilst just sitting itching their nose or something. If I am feeling devilish, I will launch into a solo porn re-enactment extravaganza, and they don't know what the hell has hit them, let alone what to do. Otherwise, if I am tired, I explain that it takes two to be dirty – they have to actually participate and give me something to work with.

Then there was the time I responded to one client's pleas for dirtiness by turning and spitting in his face. Now that could have gone any of a few ways, but thankfully his eyes lit up – I had hit the spot. He had spit running down his face. He became a regular.
Some clients just have the attitude of 'I've paid for this, and I can't be bothered to move'. Fair enough, I say, just makes my job a bit harder, that's all, but hey, that's why they pay me.

Another practicality to 'working sex' is the art, and for sure it is an art, of making the client think it's all going his way and he's getting a lot from me, and I am 'in the moment' as it were. Well…. where do I start?! Firstly, even though I say so myself, I am a good-looking woman, and I would always present myself very well; perfect hair, make-up, manicure, perfume – the full Monty and that's them on the back foot from the get-go. First bit done.

A lot of clients expect an escort to be a skank and, excuse my big-headedness here, I don't want to come over as an arse, but I could see how intimidated they were by reading their body language within seconds of meeting me. I had them in the palm of my hand, but I would never act like I knew it.
I would often find the client would nip off for a quick wash once he realised that we were maybe the type of woman he would never attempt to pull in a million years. Apparently, it's ok for a man to stink if the escort is a skank, delightful.

If I can work out what makes a particular client tick, easier if I visit him at his home and I can see his lifestyle and possessions, I get him talking about it – usually his job or car if he thinks he can impress me with either of those or just whatever he will ramble on about. This was when my great skill as an interviewer came in; I could rival Parkinson on this score. I can fire off endless questions on any boring old subject. I've kept men talking about wrestling, tyres, cars, caravan holidays, sound systems, barbeques, episodes of Columbo (which to be honest is one of my favourite shows, so that one was easily done), traffic cones, skiing, John Wayne films, bacon sandwiches, horse brasses, and spuds. In fact, you name it, I've probably had a long-drawn-out conversation with a man I do not know from Adam about it – more talk, less sex.

One client who a few of the escorts at the agency saw was a bit different, can't put my finger on why exactly, but all the other escorts at the agency liked seeing him. He was just a lovely gentle, intelligent man, like many clients, but this fella stood out, and in this book, I could make certain client's identities obvious to people who know them, but I wouldn't do that, so I'll keep it vague with this man. He was a keen astronomer and was fascinating when he talked about this subject. He always brought whichever escort he was seeing a huge cupcake which was always appreciated, but he just had something lovely about him, all the escorts agreed and none of us could understand why some woman hadn't snapped him up…he had a major tights fetish and would just ask us to wear (brand new, in the packaging) tights and feel our legs, easy peasy, cupcake, yum yum.

I am always quite surprised by how much a client will tell me about their personal life, things you would only tell those closest to you, intimate details of relationships, divorces, abuse, strange activities, the lot. To the point where I almost want to tell them they shouldn't be telling me these things. I think a lot of clients see escorts as something 'other', not quite 'real', so maybe open up to us, like you sometimes can with a stranger because they are not invested and are only getting your own side of things. But some of it is cringe-worthy and has too much information.

I know I see a different side to a lot of men to the side shared with partners. I have had the accusation levelled at me that my view of men has been skewed by my job, I always answer by suggesting that I simply see them more realistically. Men can compartmentalise their lives more easily than women, I think.

One thing that would annoy me is when they started bitching about their wives, some even show me dirty pictures of them on their phones and scoff at their figures – despicable. Almost as despicable is all the 'mansplaining'. Oh, God!! What would we silly women know if we didn't have a man to explain it all to us? In my role as a sex worker as well as just being a woman I find myself being patronised by men to the point where I could scream at the top of my lungs for hours on end out of pure anger and exasperation, maybe many of you female readers will feel the same?

In the context of sex work, the older I got in the business the more I noticed it, a presumption that a) I had NEVER done anything else than sex work and along with that they presumed sex work was somehow a piece of piss/an easy life, and b) I was bloody stupid! Honestly, the number of times I have told a client/man that I am very experienced in a certain field yet STILL have it explained to me (a few times I had sex work mansplained to me by clients who knew I had been in the business for years!) as obviously as a mere woman I didn't really understand what the hell I was talking about and don't get me started on men, especially irritating if they are 20 years younger than me calling me 'Darlin' and the more patronising 'babe'!

Incidentally, other sex-related words I cannot stand are 'pussy' and 'play'. Play being a vomit inducing euphemism for sex. One client I had nearly exploded with disbelief when he told me he was reading Goeth as part of a course he was doing, and I asked if it was Faust or some of his poetry maybe? Maybe he thought I couldn't read?

As I got older in the business it grated on me more, I was 46, perimenopausal and probably had more life experience in my little finger than they had full stop, yet they insisted I was a 'girl' or 'sweetheart'. (Granted, it is my curse that I do look shockingly young for my age... but still, I don't pass as a 'girl'). On explaining to one client why it was pissing me off that he kept calling me a girl he laughed it off (irritating in itself) and thought my objection was because I was upset that I was no longer very young and couldn't be called a girl anymore, hmmm when I asked him if at 46 he had been referred to as a 'boy' would he not have objections? This of course had never crossed his mind and he didn't seem to see what I was complaining about.

None of this was quite as irritating as many clients' response to telling them any kind of 'life story/experience' was 'bless you', sorry? Who died and made you the Pope? How some wives and girlfriends put up with that crap, I'll never know. Answers on a postcard, please! Still, it kept the clients who did it happy, I would say my piece, but leave them totally unenlightened, with cash on the hip.

The thing is, as an escort I am always 'at work', not 'having sex', so every minute of the appointment is mapped out in my head. I started to suss out clients pretty quickly once I became a pro – what's going to work, what I could get away with, or not. My old faithful is the massage, God I get away with murder with this one.

Remember, most clients are pretty nervous so offering a massage to start was usually welcomed as they didn't have a clue what else to do and meant they could just lie there and calm down a bit. My intention with the massage is just to stretch it out as long as humanly possible, just like keeping them talking. Fills time.

I start with them lying on their stomach naked, the whole time talking absolute twaddle in a slightly flirty fashion. I massage them in a very made-up way, including an arse massage. Sometimes a quick rim if I wasn't getting a whiff of stale arse crack (I once had a client whose bum hole reeked of ammonia, like an old home perm kit) I might drape my hair down their back in an oh-so-exotic style and might do the same with my hefty bosoms which always goes down very well. I kiss their back, trying to avoid big old spots and flaky patches, if there are any and sometimes, I straddle a leg and dry hump it and other vaguely stupid things.

They sometimes ask for a massage, again, totally impractical – oil gets literally everywhere, and it seems to spread at a rate of knots. You will never get rid of oil, ever! At all times my trusty watch was in full view. I liked the intro and massage to take up at least fifteen minutes, but if they are just lying there, quite happy, I just carry on, eventually asking if they are still awake/alive. Once they start to wriggle a bit, I know I can't get away with the massage any longer and I have to get on with it! Usually, I flip 'em over and they usually have a semi/stiffy, so the obvious option is BJ.   On one occasion though, the client actually came during that initial back massage…. think he had had a dry spell. I often ask the client if they wanted to give me a back massage, a good way to kill time without having to do much except wonder if I had a spot on my arse. Some are really good; a lot are clueless, and it feels awful, but I pretend it is a sensual treat so that he will carry on and not ask me to turn over and proceed to slaver all over my tits. God how I hate them touching my nipples, I feel like cracking them over the head when they do it. The thing is most of my clients have booked me for my substantial bosom and I know that, so I just have to grin and bear it. I give them about 10 seconds on each one then come up with something else that means removing my bust from their grasp.

80% of appointments run thus: massage, BJ, sex, chat, mini-BJ, some pointless attempt at more sex, goodbye, get out, relax and stop smiling immediately.

As an escort, you are in a dilemma if the client can't get an erection for whatever reason…hmmm, I need to look like I'm REALLY trying to give you a stonker, but not actually trying THAT hard, but hey I'm TRYING REALLY HARD…but please don't get hard. Hey, I'm only human, everyone likes skiving and getting an early finish at work don't they…Don't lie. One of the most tedious things in all of human existence is sucking on a flaccid cock for any longer than two minutes without a glimmer of a hard-on. Now, if I were talking about a partner here, I would have a different perspective/more sympathy, but I am not, and time is money my friend, time is money. One can feel as if one has a dead baby rat in one's gob on such occasions, and don't get me started on men 'holding back' an orgasm and thinking the escort will appreciate it or be impressed by his staying power.

Giving a client a blow job for any longer than circa 10 minutes is painfully tedious. Conjuring up images of the blow-er being akin to a slowed-down Woody Woodpecker or any pigeon you care to mention. I did comment earlier in this book that I don't 'switch off' during appointments....45-minute blowjobs are the exception! Many times, clients have wanked themselves into oblivion before their appointment so as not to embarrass themselves and last longer once they were with me, gggggggrrrrrr is all I can say to that. Two words for you my friend, 'HURRY' and 'UP'.

I sometimes offer to 'put on a show'. Clients mostly love this idea, something a bit naughty the wife or girlfriend gave up on donkey's years ago or never did full stop. My reasoning behind this is, purely practical. It extends the time when they aren't touching me. Clients taking a lot of coke often request this. Cocaine use was fairly common when I started working as an escort. Then I noticed as the recession tightened its grip it seemed to pan out a bit, but it was good for the escort as clients on coke think they can achieve a lot and pay you for hours and hours and want you to do all sorts of things like striptease because they themselves can't really manage anything. But they are always sooo hopeful and determined, bless them.

Firstly, I ask the client to sort some music, they take a while to fuss about doing that, it can take a long time to scroll through the music channels on a TV before you find suitable music to strip to. One thing is for sure, heavy metal does not work – it looks more like the stripper is possessed by the devil himself, or maybe a touch of St Vitus dance!

Once the music is decided upon, I strip or generally prance about in my knickers. I purposely do the most ridiculous moves just to entertain myself really, see what I can get away with. I remember one time when I was in a hotel room with a client, and I attached the supplied drinking glasses to my boobs via the magic of suction and struck various poses. He loved it. Warning: be very careful when removing glasses suctioned to one's boobies, no sudden movements.

There were quite a few times I dry humped household items as I stripped, chairs, bedposts, coffee tables, a massive ornamental giraffe. This all went down well with the clients and was good cardio-vascular exercise. Sometimes I'd manage some leg work too; squats are easy to work into a sexually charged dance routine I find – after all, we escorts must look after our figures.

I also offer 'poses'. If I do this within a two-girl job I have the other escort giggling her guts up, God knows what the client is doing – probably the same, whilst also thinking 'is this woman drunk'? Poses are, as you would imagine, a series of provocative positions. Some coy, some obscene, but all done with a good spirit and verve! Appealing to men's strong visual stimulation instinct, I'm not daft me, you know? Other escorts didn't seem to adopt my techniques though, something about not wanting to look like a big old fool – each to their own, I suppose. Hmm well, end up having more sex then, I say!

Another good time waster is a uniform/roleplay. Firstly, you can disappear into another room and take absolutely ages getting changed. I have a nurse, policewoman, secretary, prison officer, French maid, and a whole host of domination-style clobber. A lot of men ask for a uniform when they book, but once we were together, they forget all about it. They ask for lots of services when they book that they never actually get around to. I think they just get off on knowing they could get a woman to do 'naughty stuff', a case of eyes bigger than the belly.

I am very good at roleplay and get booked for this type of job more than most. Having almost no embarrassment threshold is a must for this type of appointment. I go into character and the client will look a bit bewildered – a lot of people are so reticent and shy about everything, not I and I won't break character until absolutely necessary.

Again, I do a lot of things to amuse myself. I come out with some amusing stuff during roleplay. I remember being in my policewoman's uniform and strutting around the client's hotel room and stopping at the window to pretend to witness a crime in progress. I radioed it into the station in a very urgent and dramatic way. The client was in stitches and the Oscar goes to…and like a script, the escort must remember her lines.

During an appointment, I talk so much twaddle and make up all sorts of personal details. I seldom tell a client anything real about myself, unless they are things that don't matter. But if and when I see them again, I have to desperately remember what I had told them the first time. After a while, I obviously just picked a story and stuck to it. I never told them my real name, if I didn't need to, if they pressed me and wouldn't shut up about it I'd pretend to give in and tell them it was Catherine (eventually I started taking payment by bank transfer so I had to tell them my name)first name that came to mind and I'd make up my home town and all other details of my life. An escort must have anonymity, I don't know who these people are and don't need them or their mates turning up at my doorstep or any other number of weird things they can do if they have my real details.

A lot of other escorts did not stick to this rule, and they were very stupid not to, I say. When I am with a client I am 'bargaining' all the time in my head, it's hard to explain, but the idea is to let the client think it is all very free and easy, spontaneous, but boy, it is far from it on my part. I have almost every move worked out ahead of time, within minutes of being with him, getting an idea of the type of things he likes, and how he has sex. It is a case of, if I give him XY and Z for three minutes each he will then want to do this that, and the other, which means I can get away with doing less of whatever neck-breaking thing he will surely then want to do because I will have ended up in such and such position by then and so on and so on. The whole time remembering to be sexy, after a while in the job I found I did forget that bit. You have to be a forward planner in this game.

I sometimes wonder how shocked my clients would be if they knew what is going on in my head while I am acting the porn star! Another little trick of mine is, when the client has about twenty minutes left in their hour-long appointment and maybe we are just chatting, I slowly start putting my clothes back on as I continue to chat casually. This gives them a cue that the appointment is coming to an end when it isn't really, is it readers?! They can still make another attempt at some sexual act, but no, because look, the escort is getting dressed. I can usually save about five or six minutes with this one and that's about five or six minutes I can stop talking rubbish, so that is worth it.

Another 'practicality classic', as all escorts know, is when a client asks you 'What's your favourite position?' All together now... 'from behind'. The reasons for this are manifold. a) you can't see them anymore, b) they can't see your face anymore, so you can drop the smile, pout, look of interest, c) a lot of men cum quicker in this position, so it gets it all over with, d) you can look at your watch openly and not out of the corner of your eye, e) you can scratch your nose/rest your eyes.

A mention must go to water sports where practicalities are concerned. Water sports – urinating on the client – is quite a common request for escorts. There's money in piss, for sure, but it's such a hassle. I only eventually started offering this service occasionally, having to remove my beloved hold-ups and have piss running down my legs, standing in my own wee-wee and the subsequent shower in some man's possibly less-than-sparkling bathtub gets old very quickly, as does the smell.

As much as I find it amusing to see one client, whose first time it is and isn't sure he likes it, realises he doesn't, oops too late, I've started so I'll have to finish. And the ones who want the flow aimed into their mouths, hmm sexy.

I've had a poo on a couple of clients (hard sports), although what is so sporty about these things, I'm not totally sure. I have done the deed and left them to it, I ain't hanging around to smell that little adventure or get any of it on me in some God-awful misreading of the situation on the part of the client and walking back to my car like a walking dirty protest! OMG, can you think of anything worse than being shat on?.......other than when you use the communal boxing gloves at your gym, and they are wet inside haha.

Now, the practicality of safe sex, which I will tell you now, men have much less awareness of than women. Women tend to be more health aware anyway in my opinion and as I said in my opening gambit, they have their brains switched on throughout the act and are therefore still capable of realising that they really don't need to end up with a case of blue waffle (Google it, if necessary) or some such debacle, for the sake of a five-minute wonder. All escorts get offers of what is called 'bareback', no condom, for more cash, usually £20 to £50 I found. Now, considering that a lot of escorts can and do earn thousands of pounds a week, waving £20 under one's nose for the prospect of catching any old STI or being impregnated by some nobody is not particularly appealing, although some escorts do offer it, which frankly boils my piss, making things harder and more dangerous for those of us who don't. Of course, it is industry standard to not use a condom for oral, known as oral without or OWO, and STIs can be transmitted thus but I accept that for the money I make. Hence, during my time as a sex worker I have had two STIs, both in my throat which for a career in sex of over 13 years I think is surprisingly few. All I can ever do is minimise my risk, but it's inherent in the job.

If the subject comes up, I honestly find that 90% of clients just presume that I do not have an STI because I look 'clean'. Hmm, yes, I have had a wash, sadly this does not now, nor has it ever prevented or cured STIs – many seem to think only skanks are capable of having a disease. I have discussions with enough clients on the topic that indicates many have a non-existent understanding of how STIs are transmitted, symptoms or lack of, long-term implications, the process of getting tested, and what the results actually mean. I can only presume they know about the birds and bees and that they are aware that the stork doesn't actually deliver babies, and Mary was not a virgin.

Any escort who hadn't sorted her own permanent contraception was asking for trouble, although I have known escorts who had aborted client's babies more than once!

It's a confidential service, but I know a lot of escorts were not honest when they attended (the agency would request to see a clean bill of STI health every two months or we couldn't work), which I can understand, but these clinics are used to seeing women working in the sex industry and in my experience don't bat an eyelid.

Although not sexually transmitted, most escorts I have known are martyrs to BV (bacterial vaginosis) and cystitis, especially if they are very busy escorts. There is so much vaginal activity if you are seeing a lot of clients, so much you come into contact with vag-wise: condoms, lubricant, fingers, tongues, sex toys, wipes, and because of this we tend to wash a lot too and it all disrupts the natural balance.

I've had clients trying to quickly whip condoms off when they think you can't see so they could shag me without one. That is the only real drawback to the 'from behind' position really. It is easiest for them to do it in that position, hence I always reach around and put their cock in myself (yes, I do have hyper-flexible shoulders and eyes in the back of my head, before you ask). They ALWAYS 'just want to rub it (their UNCONDOMMED dick) against me (my vag)' as if this activity is completely consequence-free, ggggrrrr.

When I first started in the job, I was lying back with my eyes closed (a rookie mistake but I was trying to look like I was enjoying it and in gay abandon), while a client busied himself between my legs. I presumed with his hands, but I happened to look up and he was merrily rubbing his semi on my fan. I freaked out and he nearly jumped out of his skin, eyes bulging cartoon-style. Idiot! I gave him a lecture and a half. I mean honestly, some men need to read a pamphlet!! An escort has to have eyes not only in the back of her head but just about everywhere, it's exhausting!

Most of these men have partners and I've had only two clients over the years working as an escort ask for a condom for a BJ. That will be because they had partners and were actually showing them a bit of respect by not wanting their cheating behaviour to result in giving them a disease and that was probably more to do with them not getting found out than concern for the poor woman's health.

Lastly in this chapter on practicality is the very practical subject of periods. Most escorts, myself included, have come on a period mid-appointment. In my case, the few times I did were just a case of coming on my period days early, totally out of the blue. It happens, no big deal. I would always apologise to the client, especially if he got himself covered in it, oops, and ask him how he wanted to play it, especially if it was early on in the appointment. I personally am never ashamed or anything like that; you book a woman to have sex with, you get a woman, women have periods, and I cannot predict if I'm going to be early, can I? Most men are fine about it in general, with a few freaked-out exceptions, I once had a client move away from me and proceed to treat me like I was contagious and unclean, couldn't get rid of me fast enough, which in this day and age I found odd. It's not a pleasant thing to happen for either party, but he needed to step out of the sixteenth century maybe. I offer clients appointments offering limited services during my period which some are happy to do but I did have one client who liked to have sex when I was bleeding, didn't matter to me, I went to his house for the booking, so it was him left with a duvet cover like a murder scene after, not I.

A lot of escorts shove a piece of sponge up themselves when they are on their period to stem the flow, but I say, just have a few days off, darling, a sponge up the vag cannot be good for you. I used to find sponges with bits ripped out all over the agency flats, which was just bad housekeeping at the end of the day.

In conclusion, a good escort has to give the impression of wild abandon, whilst actually having the mindset of a general about to go into battle; a tough combo, I think you will agree.

CHAPTER 5

IT'S A FUNNY SAD MAD WORLD

As an escort, you get to witness all human life, if you do it long. I've been in many heart-breaking and upsetting situations where I've had to be some sort of social worker or counsellor and I know most other escorts have too.

I have, of course, seen clients who have been nasty and tried to treat me like shit, mainly because I refused to perform a certain act, totally justifiably, I might add.

Like the man with the razor-sharp, jaggedly teeth whose face I wouldn't sit on. Let me tell you, I would have been cut to ribbons and maybe a tetanus injection would have been needed, who knows? He then went on to treat me like crap and splatted his lumpen cum in my face after he gave himself a hand job as his parting shot. He hadn't said a word since I had politely refused to perform that particular service, I was obviously not worth talking to now. He did, however, bark his final thoughts, something like 'useless fucking whore'; nice one, Jaws! I had been as polite as I was able throughout the appointment, and you have to understand as an escort you have to be circumspect and not let a situation escalate. I was alone with a man I did not know; I couldn't risk making matters worse; even though it used to kill me to keep my mouth shut.

You also have to consider that clients can leave reviews of escorts on various punter sites. Some punters can be total bitches with nothing better to do frankly and these reviews spread like wildfire, so it's not worth it.

There are a couple of occasions that really stick out that

were particularly sad. I had been booked for a job and the fella taking the bookings at the time had asked me if I minded seeing an eighty-five-year-old – the client had asked him to make the potential escort aware of his age. I said I didn't mind; this job was a job for me, practical, it's not a date and to be honest the really old clients always have the kettle on and some biscuits on the go – unlike the younger men. Many clients don't even offer a drink of water when I turn up, sometimes I can put this down to nerves, but sometimes just ignorance, I'm a guest, you fool! So, the elderly score points there simply because making tea and doling out biccies takes up a good fifteen minutes of the appointment, score!

Anyway, I drove to the client's house – all in a day's work and there he was waiting for me at the front door, hanging off a zimmer frame, smiling. Now my boss used to ask how we could see clients like this, really meaning any client who wasn't 'average' youngish, OK looking, not hitting ninety, but that's a man or maybe a non-escort's viewpoint. They think because it's a sexual job, it's a sexual experience for the escort, but it's not; it's a job of work. Simple as that.

I cannot talk for all sex workers, but I always switch to actress mode with all clients, and I've had some stunning clients, in great shape, attractive in lots of different ways but in 14 years of this job I can honestly say, I never found one single client desirable. For me, it does not matter how attractive they are, it's the fact that they are prepared to pay for sex, they buy into my crap, it's a massive turn-off. If I knew I had another client straight after another then, given the choice, I would prefer seeing the old man first as opposed to possibly some young buck as I am not going to get ragged around for the whole appointment, potentially leading to sweatiness and disarranged make-up and hair to then have to go on to see someone else.

I digress. This old chap – let's call him Bert – was waiting for me in his cardigan. I walked up the path and smiled, introduced myself and went inside. As the escort, I was professional, polite, trying to put him at ease, as they were generally more nervous than me, but the woman in me, the woman in her mid-thirties whose oldest client to date had probably been late sixties before this, was conflicted.

As the real me, I would never have seen a man so old as sexual, I mean he had obviously been sexual in his life, had partners, but he wasn't a sexual being to me. It's a huge leap to take to be sexual with someone like this; you know it's your job, you agreed to take it, you also know you can make your excuses, headache or whatever and go and there would be no dire consequences – awkwardness sure, but that would be that. I was, however, very aware that this is a human being with feelings, so why should he be penalised for getting old? It happens to the best of us!

The whole time these conflicting thoughts were swirling around your mind you must always remember to be good company, smile, be chatty, do what he was paying for, all the while feeling a bit sad at the whole situation, for him and for myself. These are feelings and situations I wouldn't bother to try to explain to non-escorts after a while, they would just look horrified and grossed out. After a while, I would only talk about such things with escorts. Like any job or walk of life, it takes one to know one and an escort can talk to another escort about clients and experiences in a way you just can't with someone outside your profession.

Back to Bert, with haste, poor old bugger. There he was, in his council-adapted bungalow and there was I in my hold-up stockings and lovely peachy lip gloss, talking total rot, as was my way and we proceed to his sitting room for, you guessed it, tea and biccies, yeah!

There were photos all around the room of him and a woman, obviously his wife and I soon discovered that she had died about five years earlier, after fifty years of marriage. Now, I have never been married, nor had the desire to be, but I find it very upsetting to imagine after having loved and shared your life with someone for fifty years they just are no more and you are left looking at an empty chair, in the house you shared with them.

Bert told me a bit about her and about his career that took

them to live in several different countries. They had a child who was now middle aged and living in a different part of the country. He told me how he was lonely and craved a woman's company and touch and I was very moved, who knows how we are all going to end up in twenty, thirty, or forty years? Who am I to judge what he wants, what we all want and need – human companionship and touch. He was hardly going to go out on the pull, was he, so what choice did he have?

So, my job was to give him a pale imitation of what he actually wanted, which was his wife back, I suppose. To be honest, I understood and could excuse this type of client much more than a man who could possibly go out and actually meet women for real – get a woman who actually wanted him.

Disabled clients are another case in point. I've seen men who are paralysed or immobile, they want sex, but many times are not in any position to go out and do it the usual way, so what choice do they have? It was often the carer or mother of these disabled clients who rang to book, but not always. Suppose it depended on how mobile/independent the client was. If it had been booked by someone else on the client's behalf, then when I arrived at their house, they would let me in and go into another room to watch "Coronation Street" or some such. Their charges were young men and young men want sex, simple as, so it's an easy practical solution.

One carer used to drop off the lad he was looking after at whichever agency flat we were using; helped me get him out of his wheelchair then go over the road to the pub and come back in an hour. The client went back in the wheelchair and was off into the night – job done. A lot of escorts would cringe at seeing a disabled client, but to me they were perfect, they weren't going to be all over me – win-win. By the way, being paralysed from the waist down does not always stop a man's penis from functioning sexually…I did not know that…did you?

I did have one paralysed client who was always dressed up as something different every time I saw him. His carer would dress him in whatever he desired, a woman, a bondage gimp, and worryingly, a baby. Now it's tricky when things like that happen because, although I would never pretend to be underage/calling clients Daddy and all that crap, but here I was with a disabled adult in a baby's bonnet, hmm. That kind of thing has only happened once in my whole time as an escort and I just play it by ear, I wait and find out what is required of me first, but I never do anything against my principles in these circumstances. As far as I recall he didn't even refer to how he was dressed and if he wasn't going to, why should I? If he had wanted anything I wasn't comfortable with I would have just politely refused. Although I do remember almost losing a vibrating butt plug up his arse one visit, as he didn't have the best muscle control. Thank God they have a little lip on the bottom of them...It saved a trip to A and E, that's for sure.

Anyway, we must get back to Bert. It's time to go to the bedroom. I am well aware that a client like Bert is not going to be up for bedroom gymnastics and a mammoth session, so it's all going to be pretty limited, and it was. He just wanted to lie down and have me sit over his face, he wanted to feel me up between my legs and as far as I remember we tried sex, but it wasn't going to happen for him, so I made him cum with my hand, a kind of 'Last of the Summer Wine' situation if you see my point?

Very tame stuff, but it took all my 'strength of character' if that's the correct way to put it, to get through it. Yes, I'm a sex worker, but first and foremost I'm a normal woman and I don't want to get sexual with the elderly. IT'S DISGUSTING.

But, at the end of the day, I would always rather do something weird or extreme for an hour than something tediously drawn out and soul destroying for a whole week, like most regular jobs, for the same money. Even if it does involve looking directly into someone's stoma bag as it filled up with poo, as I sucked them off.

I was very glad when it was over, all ten minutes of it and we were back amongst the doilies in his sitting room. We talked for a little while about something and nothing, but the whole time all I could think about was how vulnerable he had made himself.

He didn't know me from Adam; I could have bashed his brains in and ransacked his house or had a boyfriend waiting outside to do it. In being so lonely he was laying himself wide open and I felt like staying longer, talking more, like being a counsellor. But I had to remind myself that he was just a client like any other. He may not have wanted special treatment, he may have wanted me to get lost, he had had his hour and a half, and I had to be professional, no blurred lines, black and white, best way.

Another client that sticks in my memory was a young lad, maybe early twenties. He had opted to have his appointment at one of the city centre flats. Let's call him John, in honour of all the clients who feel the need to give a false name. They always picked Dave or Steve and Asian men picked Tony, for some reason. Anyhoo, this particular John was a big fat lad; fat as he was tall, I discovered on opening the front door.

I greeted him with my winning 'here we go a-bloody-gain smile' and led him to the bedroom. He sat on the bed, and we chatted. He was shy and nervous, but I needed to get out of the client what he wanted, or I would run the risk of sitting and talking for the whole appointment. Some of these bitchy clients would report an escort to the agency for anything. If THEY had been too nervous to ask for what they wanted, you could find yourself with a bad review.

I had a client once who had a skin disease and we discussed what I was prepared to actually do with him – considering he was flaking all over the shop! We came to a friendly agreement, and I proceeded to tease him with a riding crop I had to hand – probably in just knickers, hold-ups, heels and tits out, I would imagine, and touched the non-flaky parts with as much sensuality as anyone could really. He seemingly went away happy. Well, he wasn't. He wrote a long and winding negative review of me and the appointment, claiming I had poked him with a stick for an hour! One question for you, – why didn't you stop me poking you with a stick then, why sit there and be a pokee for a whole hour? I swear they have nothing better to do.

Back to John. I soon got the gist he wanted the girlfriend

experience, GFE as, I concluded, he had never had one. I find that extremely overweight clients rarely take their tops off during sex, which is fair enough and John didn't either. The only position option with a man that big was for me to be on top and I would pray they didn't want anything else as the logistics are just too awkward. As it was, being on top was pretty precarious as your knees don't touch the mattress when the man's belly is that big. It was like riding a mechanical bull, only sober and trying to look seductive...tiring! I usually 'like' seeing really fat clients as they can't really do much, it's all quite limited so it's less bother.

John enjoyed himself and afterward, as we dressed, he told me how he was meeting the lads in town for a booze up. I just knew he wasn't – he wasn't dressed for it, for a start, but having been a very fat girl in a previous life, I knew the bullshit. I knew about trying to fit in and convince people of things, lying, while just sad and this was coming off him in waves. I can still see him waddling to the lift doors as he left. He wanted a woman's touch, female attention, but he had to pay for it, he paid me, it was my job, I didn't care about him to all intents and purposes, was acting, could see through him, went home and had a shower to get his smell (which was not bad, I feel I must add!) off me.

In the 'mad' category I think I would have to put the 'stuck record' fantasy brigade. These are clients that when I see them for the first time, will tell me a particular fantasy, we would act it out and that would be that. Right, great, but then the next time I saw them they would act as if they had never met me and tell me the same fantasy...this threw me off the first time it happened, but like everything in escorting, it becomes all in a day's work, which this scenario did as it's quite common.

The first time it happened was with a fat slobbish, basically-educated man who told me he was a doctor – hmm, 'I don't think you are but, whatever', was my thought. He then went on to tell me he had just split up from his wife of twenty years, his childhood sweetheart. He had never been with anyone else and was very nervous. I am sat there nodding, head tilted slightly to the side, thinking, 'BORING!' as he explains that he has booked an escort to experiment, see what another woman feels like. OK guy, good for you, we do the deed and that's that.

Well, it wasn't, because about four months later he booked me again, 'Hello,' says I, smiling and waiting for a 'Hello again, my dear,' or some such, which never came. Anyway, as we chatted he proceeded to tell me he was a doctor, and no, he still didn't pull that one off, I'm thinking erm yeah, I know, but anyway, I let him talk as you know by now reader, that is my way, and he went on to give me the same old childhood sweetheart guff and how he had never been with another woman and I'm thinking well you fucked me four months ago, so that's crap for a start, but anyway let's see where he's going with this sweet tale. Well, he was going nowhere with it, that's when it dawned on me that this was just what some men get off on, and like a sleepwalker, it's best not to wake them from their stupor or God knows what would happen.

He returned about three more times with the same story and a total lack of acknowledgement of the situation. I see quite a few clients like this, and they never acknowledge the reality of the situation at any point in the appointment. It is very odd. I just couldn't imagine a woman doing that, it's a male trait to get hung up on something sexually, like a weirdly specific fetish or repetitive fantasy, I think.

I sometimes used to ask clients who had fetishes if they could remember what had triggered them. One man I remember could only get aroused if I wore high-waisted bikini bottoms, very specifically high-waisted, none of them ever could remember, only saying they had ALWAYS had it. The presumption being little boys are very impressionable so if you are raising one at present be bloody careful, it could cost him a fortune in escort services when he's older.

When a client has a fetish though it makes the job a lot easier. Firstly, they know exactly what they want, so I don't have to use a brain cell and secondly, they are always very, very, very grateful, which is because they've probably had so many partners refusing to indulge them. Actually, most of the time the fetish they enjoy is a massive secret they have never divulged to a living soul and they ALL thought that it would be the first time I had been asked to perform it…it never is. Well apart from the first time I was asked to perform it, you get the gist. Anyway, it takes a lot to repulse me…if I'm getting paid, that is, so I just crack on! Also, I find they never stay the full hour, once they've had their fix and cum, they are usually off, toodle pip, ma dear. One fetish client used to like to ride around his bungalow on my back like I was a little horse. The first time I saw him and had assumed the position, i.e., hands and knees on his sitting room carpet, (he did supply knee pads, no way I could have done the job without them) I caught a glimpse of myself on his patio door windows, skirt, stockings, heels, topless, knee pads, small man on my back, and I did question my life choices a wee bit. What were other middle-aged women doing on a Sunday afternoon pray tell…. not this presumably. Then I got the giggles and cracked on, Beecher's Brook, here I come! As I have particularly pretty feet, I therefore put a few feet pictures on my profile to attract foot fetishists.

Now, I already knew a few niches within the foot fetish world, such as men who like high arches, which I have, and men who particularly like the wrinkles on the sole of a foot when it is pointed or shoe dangling, which is just as it sounds, dangling a shoe off a barefoot, so I do get my share of foot fetishists. Most ask for foot wanks, foot worship and ultimately want to cum on my feet. I do get requests for smelly, sweaty feet, but I do not suffer from these afflictions and wouldn't like to disappoint, otherwise easy work.

One client who became quite the regular was a man who was a good looker, and very strange. He used to lie on his stomach on a duvet he would put down on his sitting room floor and get me to lie on his back with my full weight on his, he insisted on that. He'd then instruct me to reach around, hook my fingers up his nose and yank upwards to make his nose bleed. He bloody loved it. I would always check he didn't have a cold beforehand though.

We used to lie like that and watch old pop videos on YouTube too. I particularly remember watching Go West's 'We Close Our Eyes' and eighties Europop starlet Sabrina's, 'Boys, Boys,

Boys' videos. I had to be careful not to fall off him though.

He had a fingernail fetish too, always requesting dark nail varnish, and loved pressing my long nails to test how strong they were. Hand fetishists always seemed to have a thing about strong nails, they love pressing them to test their strength, for whatever reason.

He was also a feeder. Once I said I was on a diet, I'd gained a few pounds. He got upset, holding back the tears. He left the house and went to the shop. I didn't know where the hell he had gone – I just browsed through his bookshelf to pass the time, I mean, it was his house, he had to come back. I had the feeling he needed to go to the cash machine anyway. He did finally return with a huge bar of chocolate. I said I'd eat it with a nice cuppa once I got in – it went straight into a random wheelie bin on my way home. God, I was on a diet!

We also used to look at websites selling PVC items, as he wanted me to don a black catsuit and jump out at him ninja style when he came home after a night shift! Firstly, I am not hiding behind your shed and under your clothesline at 6am in a no doubt bloody uncomfortable PVC catsuit for any amount of money. And secondly, if I were to buy a catsuit it would be alone, in private.

A lot of men seem to think if a woman isn't 'fat' she's a size ten. I've had so many clients buy me gifts in a size ten with absolutely no chance of ever fitting. I wasn't a size ten, I was a size fourteen and the only size woman who would find a catsuit that fit well and easily would be a size six, a small six at that, a small six with no arse – fact.

Anyway, that ninja thing was just one of those fantasies, a stuck record thing that would never happen. A lot of clients do it – bang on about some fantasy, never meaning for it to happen. I would keep agreeing and nodding my head, knowing it was never ever going to happen. Thank God, as a lot of them would be just stupid and embarrassing for us both.

The closest this client and I got to any kind of ninja action was once when he realised I was physically very strong, he had the bright idea to ask me to hide behind his open bedroom door with the lights out. When he wandered in, in a very 'I have absolutely no idea there's an escort hiding behind my bedroom door' type way, I was to pounce out at him, knock him to the floor and, I think, as far as I can recall, wrestle womanfully with him.

Well, not being a particularly violent person, I had no idea how to knock someone over really, so just ended up jumping on him – arms and legs wrapped around his neck and waist and just kind of stood like that for what seemed like minutes but was probably just a few seconds. We both just burst out laughing as I gracefully slid down to the floor. I still have a little giggle about that even now…when there's nothing on the telly.

The thing was with this fella, things took an uncomfortable turn. He had mentioned certain things about his dad and an incident on one Christmas day, at first, he was quite vague, but he kept adding more every time I saw him. I was building up a picture that something disturbing had happened, he was very cryptic on the subject. But, I mean, wanting someone to give you a bloody nose isn't normal and in such a specific way, eventually he asked me if I would have sex with his dad, I mean not in reality. I gathered his dad was probably dead, but it made me uncomfortable, and I just used to brush it off. Then he asked if I would kill his dad, he implied it as if a fantasy, so he could brush it off if I was outraged, but he kept asking and, in a way, I'm sure it was turning him on.

Something very serious had gone wrong in his childhood; it was as if he was testing the waters every time I saw him. I had to tell him to stop talking about it – it wasn't appropriate. As an escort you get glimpses of quite disturbing histories that come to light because the situation is sexual for the client and unreal, outside of real life, I suppose, but I had to be professional. I'm not trained to cope with such complex problems, nor did I want to. All I could do was sensitively suggest talking to someone who was and leave it there.

One male/female couple I remember used to book me regularly for a while, well, it was the wife (let's call her Sally) who was booking really. She used to save up the cash for the booking

SEX IS HARD WORK

in a biscuit tin on top of the fridge. On my first visit to their flat she said she wanted me to tell her if she was a lesbian. Hmm, why don't you know yourself, you are about forty-five, was my thought, but never mind.

She had one girl-on-girl experience at school and had never gotten over it, by the sounds of it. She'd married a man in the meantime and got on with her biscuit addiction, but she felt like a possible lesbian it seemed, so it was escort to the rescue! Being the world expert on human sexuality that I am! I of course didn't have a bloody clue if she was a lesbian or not and was not about to ponder the question.

I do remember she had drawn up a fairly extensive list of things she wanted to do with me or any woman, perfect, a client who knew exactly what they wanted during the appointment was half the battle, so a bullet pointed list was a God send.

All the way through the list the vagina was referred to as a 'fanny', which was quaint and the list of activities was written as if a thirteen-year-old girl had written them, actually. How old was that list?!

The main one she wanted to try was 'rubbing fannies together', as she put it, so we cracked on, husband and dog left sitting watching 'Britain's Got Talent', while we retreated to the bedroom next door. I will always remember I had been requested by this woman to be as close to hairless between my legs as possible. I refuse to go completely hairless, as some clients would request, as I find it creepy – taking on the look of a child, maybe in their eyes. As an escort, you always have to be on your toes regarding these matters, giving clients the benefit of the doubt about such things is not advisable in my considerable experience and as an escort you ALWAYS have to refuse anything that makes you uncomfortable, it's never worth breaking that rule I have found.

I had seen many escorts boast of having 'no taboos' or 'no limits' in their adverts, presumably to get the most work, but it's folly, very naïve and could get said escort into bother. An escort MUST have rules and limits she sticks to like glue, and if she really does have no limits or boundaries, she's as bad as the clients she's catering to, by indulging in these sickening perversions. It's quite common to get requests from clients asking you to do daddy-daughter role play or asking you to pretend to be their mothers or acting out rape or underage fantasies. I never entertain any of that shit. I've done stints of 'sex texting' when clients pay for dirty SMS messaging and got a lot of men messaging about disgusting crap. Asking if I had ever fucked a family member or animal and using the word 'rape' was fairly common as if it were an acceptable substitute for describing rough sex.

That makes me sick that there are so many men out there who just don't get it. I think they also think the rules don't apply when texting a sex worker, as if they don't have to be tiresomely socially acceptable like when communicating with 'nice' women, and it actually saddens me that I know there are sex workers out there who will not draw the line, therefore encouraging this filth.

I have come across clients who can be very subtle and sly when making requests, testing the waters, I suppose. I always have to question their motives; I'd learned that from the phone sex work I had done previously. I always refuse a request to wear my hair in a ponytail or bunches, again they are child-like styles. Maybe the requests are totally innocent, but I am certainly not going to give them the benefit of the doubt, not worth it.

I personally didn't get many dubious requests like that at the agency, as my look is very womanly and I was older than a lot of the other escorts, so not the type a client with those interests would choose, although I was always shocked how many escorts would be happy to dress up as a school girl or put on 'big' knickers, like kids knickers really and act younger than they were at the request of a client. I don't know how they could face themselves and take money for that.

Anyway, I recall Sally's fanny hair was long and silken, so she hadn't afforded me the same consideration. She had a cheek didn't she, reader?! I mean, there was a lot of it. What was I to find in there, Shergar, Lord Lucan, a biscuit?

I used to get quite a few requests to grow my pubic hair

into a 'Joy of Sex' style. I never did as it was otherwise a pretty unpopular look.

Anyway, Sally. I think first off the bat was the rubbing of the two fannies from her extensive and slightly weird list. Another of the bullet points was she wanted to drag her face right down my naked body.... erm ok, just once or repeatedly? I was presuming she meant the front of my body too, but who knew with this woman?

She had difficulty getting into certain positions, as her flexibility was poor. She honestly needed to work on that, lesbian or not. We worked our way down the list over a few appointments and she was no closer to making a decision about her leanings.

Her husband once asked to watch for half an hour, so I charged him £50 and he just sat in the corner of the bedroom, motionless. I drew the line at him bringing the dog in too. To be honest, when I get a request from a male /female couple for a threesome, I always feel a bit sad and confused that the female of the partnership wants to book an escort. A man you expect it of, but a woman surely has the nouce to know a sex worker just wants the money. How can a woman be taken in like a man on this point? I couldn't pay for sex in a million years. The only reason sex is sexy or worth doing is because the other person desires you, it's mutual, otherwise, why bother?

There was one client quite a few of the women working at the agency saw; I can't recall much of the appointment really, only that it would last literally for hours and consist of him stripping topless, jeans only, and wanking furiously while I just watched and he called me Jane. He either fancied some forbidden fruit, probably his sister-in-law, named Jane or he had a Tarzan complex. What I do know is, that by the end of the appointment his jeans were sodden with sweat to the thighs and his copious pre-cum had been whipped into a bubbly fountain. In my opinion, there is nothing more unattractive than bubbly pre-cum (or in fact any pre-cum, its stickiness gets everywhere, and it tastes like sucking on a stock cube) well sweaty jeans aren't great either, let's be honest. As I recall he resembled the TV presenter Keith

Chegwin but with a curly perm.

A weird situation in my experience many escorts have found themselves in was being booked by a gay-acting male client. I have had just a handful of such appointments and it's very odd. All the sure-fire tricks we rely on as women, things we just know work with a straight man fly out of the window, you are impotent! I just felt silly and, to be honest, a bit apologetic, as in a 'Sorry, I just haven't got what you want, ain't got the bits' sort of way. But, then again, I thought, 'Well, you booked, you could see from my profile I wasn't a big strapping lad, so let's just get on with it'. I still couldn't shake the feeling of being Superman when he comes across kryptonite. I felt that all my powers were gone!! Those clients wouldn't actually tell you they were gay; it was just obvious. Don't ask me why they booked and don't doubt they were gay, oh, they were. One such client had a cockapoo dog called Prada...not a straight man – fact.

We escorts would sometimes discuss these clients – possible motives, denial, boredom, experimentation, too much money, too much time, loneliness, and self-loathing. None of us ever asked any of them – didn't want to get into it, and if they wanted to pay for sex with a woman that was up to them – always got better chat from a gay client anyway.

A mention must go to 'Mr. Deal or No Deal'. He had come to the region from elsewhere in the country for a 'Deal or No Deal', the quiz show audition the next day and I went to see him at his hotel.

He let me into his room. He was very fat, yeah, no gymnastics! I started the act; lights, camera, action. Once we were on the bed, him naked, me between his legs... I realised that I couldn't find his cock!!! His fat was so all encompassing I couldn't see a thing genitals-wise, not a ball, not a tip, not a pube. I ended up pretending to tease him, hoping he liked that kind of thing while I kept hunting and getting into a small panic as I realised I may have to ask him where his cock was. I REALLY didn't want to go there! No client wants to be asked that!

I am quite strong and was often to be found merrily chin

upping in my local gym, so I decided that I was going to have to 'raise the canopy'. It simply had to be there. The man had already told me he had children, so he must have had one at one point and as far as I know, he would be aware if it had dropped off since.

So, with one big old heave-ho, I pushed the belly up. It weighed a ton but then there was the 'fat of the mound', the only way I can put it, to cope with it was a two-arm job, but there it was, or at least I think it was. It was just a nubbin, really, and so as I wasn't one hundred percent sure it was a penis, I decided to leave go of the mound with one arm and start on the nubbin to see if it responded. It did, and thankfully it was all over quite quickly as my arm taking the strain was giving way and starting to shake – good upper body exercise that if anyone in reader land is looking for one.

I've had quite a few obese clients like that, and it never gets any easier to find the penis. Weirdly enough, practice does not make perfect in that situation, just gotta keep on keepin' on.

One amusing incident I still have a little titter about is the client I visited in a smart city centre hotel. He had requested an escort happy to perform domination, so off I went, my 'dirty bag' in hand.

Now, I don't think I've mentioned my dirty bag thus far – it is a bag of tricks I keep in the back of my car. Not to be taken on the average job, but for any client who requests domination, toys, gadgets, like a butt plug or strap on; both of which we escorts would cover with a condom for hygiene, as well as my dildo – which is in my everyday escorting kit – it's never out of service, that thing. I have my uniforms and some whips and chains type clobber in the dirty bag too, so it came on this job with me.

I met the client and we chatted about what he wanted, and he then said he wanted to go into the bathroom to put on a suitable outfit and that I too should pick something appropriately kinky and get changed in the bedroom. Right, fine.

I picked out a black fishnet crotchless catsuit with domination style straps over the bust and up to my neck I had recently bought, black shiny 'fuck me' heels and voila – quite a look! Well, he must have agreed, as he emerged from the bathroom in exactly the same outfit, although his shoes were not up to the job, being more like court shoes your Grandmama might wear for a tea dance. The thing is crotchless catsuits are generally made for women only for a reason, a flaccid, grey fuzzy-pubed penis is not made any more attractive for hanging out of a crotchless anything – never mind a catsuit. Maybe you think differently, but that's up to you. He took it in good spirits, but hope he rinsed it through when he got home. I quite often see clients who dress in women's underwear, for most men this is not a good look, too many knobbly knees in sheer stockings and hairy shoulders for my liking.

I remember one client who made me want to jump out of the window with sheer desperation though. He had seen quite a few of the escorts at the agency, he had quite significant cerebral palsy symptoms, which we briefly discussed, but that's for later in the story. He booked me at one of the work flats for three hours. Hmm, good money but I hated long appointments, potential yawn fest.

Anyway, turns out he had no patter or chat, talking to him was like getting blood out of a flaming stone or pulling teeth. I did, after about an hour, wrangle out of him that he worked in the world of sprockets or some such boring thing, working in his dad's firm. Right, OK, I didn't know much about sprockets, and he was in no way forthcoming on the subject. By this point I was getting a bit panic stricken as we still had hours of this appointment left and I had almost exhausted every single topic known to escort kind, so in my immense wisdom I suggested that he try to impress his dad by writing a report or dossier on the state of the sprocket industry around the world, for example, Finland?!? Don't ask. I literally could not stop myself from talking, the voice in my head was screaming at me to shut up, but I just couldn't.

I then found myself telling the client I had invented a jetpack to beat the rush hour traffic!!! How my legs dangled over people's heads as I floated jet propelled above their stationary cars, vans, motorbikes, lorries, buses, tricycles, limousines, you

SEX IS HARD WORK

get the picture. I literally could not stop babbling. It was then, as I gabbled, I was trying to work out how much physical damage jumping out of a second story window could actually do, and I was quite serious about weighing it up. The fact that I was 'dressed' only in hold-up stockings and heels worried me not, it was summer anyway, so everyone was scantily clad. I might have blended right in.

To add insult to injury he had accused me of breaking his cock, what joy! I had not broken the man's cock, he just overreacted to a weirdly tightening foreskin situation. How is that MY fault?! I saw him again a few months later, yes, he booked AGAIN, God knows why, maybe he wanted to see how my jetpack patenting was coming along. His cerebral palsy symptoms were very much reduced though, so I commented on this. He however, in a bizarre move, denied ever having cerebral palsy. Well, by then my friend, I knew when to just shut up and let a client believe what they wanted. And to be honest, I was too preoccupied trying to summon up a list of possible subjects to raise during our next three hours together. It was hard as I had already exhausted all my jetpack chat in our previous encounter.

Yes, the long appointment, the escort must weigh up the potential money to be earned with having to find a usually, fairly boring man interesting for hours on end, and almost literally dying of boredom. For me the sex in a long appointment is not a consideration, as I've said, hey that's the job, it's gross but at least they have stopped talking at that point, to be honest, there can be the same amount of sex in an hour's job as a three-hour job, most clients are not Olympic athletes! How many three- or four-hour jobs have I done where the client has espoused mildly racist/ sexist/everyone different to "him-ist" views and got more and more right wing and boring as the appointment went on. Doing that thing some men do when they talk AT you rather than engage in a conversation, heaven forbid the 'listener' should interject spontaneously and stem their flow! I find they simply bide their time with an impatient/annoyed look on their faces until you have shut up and they can carry on their monologue and teach you things. I would argue the toss as much as I could be bothered but I had to remember I was being paid and just wanted to go home. Taking the long job to extremes was the potential of a foreign holiday with a client. I got asked to do this a few times.

NO WAY JOSE! Firstly, the client often couched this offer in a way that presumed I was poverty stricken, (lots of clients make this assumption I find...hmm my hourly rate is probably many times more than yours so why presume that please sir?) Secondly, they are living in a dream world. Why would you want to commit yourself to a full week or so with a woman you do not know from Adam? Oh sorry, we had an hour together where I was all tarted up, faking orgasms, yes, I forgot.

Presumably they did not realise I am, in reality, quite a miserable middle-aged woman who, 15 minutes after waking, is plucking her chin? My hair, my spirits, and my armpits do not do well in hot weather, and I avoid it most of the time, add to that mix, a sweaty virtual stranger eager for sex and other weirdness and you have a recipe for pure misery and secretly googling flights for one back home.

One odd request I got from a client was to supply him with used condoms, with as much spunk still in as possible. The mind boggles! I refused because a) how on earth do you harvest them? Whip said used condom off, tout suite, put a paper clip at the top and pop into some bedside Tupperware, all the while smiling benignly at the client and b) I got it into my head that the contents could be planted at crime scenes to incriminate innocent people or whatever. But then again, I watch a lot of crime dramas on TV.

I have been asked to be filmed walking around a supermarket, standing next to unsuspecting shoppers and farting (it's a 'thing' if you don't know). Again, I refused because a) it was too public and indiscreet not, to say ridiculous and b) who can fart on command? I did think maybe I could just make the noise orally and move on, but I really do have better things to do.

Mr. Tickle was an agency regular – he would bring a little pouch of brushes, like artist's paint brushes to tickle us with, it's hard faking girlish giggles for forty-five minutes, I can tell you, especially whilst wondering if he had washed his paint brushes lately.

There was also the client who had requested a strap-on. I had just bought a new one as my last one had 'gone missing'. In reality, a client had probably taken it as a souvenir. So, I took myself off to the bathroom to put it on, but realised it tilted off to the left in a marked fashion. I fiddled about with it for ages, getting a light panicked changing room type sweat on, to try and get it to face front, but it just wouldn't cooperate. So, as I strode confidently back into the bedroom, I gripped the shaft in what looked like a sexually charged and menacing stance, but in reality, I was just getting it to look the client in the eye. A bit ridiculous but then again, who doesn't look bloody ridiculous wearing a strap-on? I spent the whole appointment adopting stances where it would tilt back the right way – exhausting. On further inspection I found it was a bent dong, faulty goods! I thought about asking for my money back for it but couldn't face that conversation in store!

I remember one client asking me for dirty talk, this is quite a regular request and I had never had any complaints before, so I launched into it all – porn star crap that always worked…well not always, as this particular client was just watching me with a look of what can only be described as pity mixed with boredom. After a minute or so of me rambling on, he asked me to stop; wrinkled his nose and shook his head. I found this amusing and was glad of it as you don't half run out of things to say when talking dirty, don't you find?

I've played a game of naked pool with a client. Well, I kept my hold-ups and heels on as per usual – partly to look sexier but also to make sure I could see over the pool table, as I wasn't the tallest escort going.

I remember one occasion being booked by a couple to film them having sex, a homemade porn film. I duly obliged, stretching and straining to get creative angles and reaction shots, move over Mr. Martin Scorsese, there's a new kid in town.

A mention must go to 'The Veg Man'. I don't think he got five a day, but he certainly got a couple. I would go to his house for bookings, a nice house in a pleasant street and when I walked in, I would see what was on today's menu, vegetables. He was a big fan of cucumbers and parsnips, but the stew pot often included carrots and celery. The celery was presumably for texture but we found celery did not have the tensile strength of the parsnip when rammed up the bum, while he told me of his 'big transsexual hooker' fantasy. Dignity, always dignity.

Oh, and I must mention my first client, Jim, remember him? Mr. Girlfriend Experience. Well, a few years later he booked me again and he now wanted to eat my shit, literally, whilst being verbally humiliated. He wanted me to have control of his finances, money pig style. For God's sake, what happened to you Jim?? One job was with a client in his 60s I would estimate. He had been married and presumably had a few other sexual partners, thing is his genitals looked exactly like a face and nobody had ever told him. When he flipped over after his massage it was the first thing I saw was a cock nosed face! He had two large symmetrical birthmarks 'eyes', said cock nose, finished off with a very smooth semi-circular line under his ball sack, a smile! I wondered why it hadn't been his party piece at every drunken occasion he had ever been to?

There was the client in his fifties who would spend what seemed like hours…Oh wait, it WAS hours, dry humping my leg in various positions, all the while grinning at me like a looney and turning bright red. Well I ask you! His wife had recently left him, I know that would come as a surprise to you readers…Trying to come up with appropriate facial expressions in a situation like that is tough, challenging! All you can do for sure is keep eye contact to a minimum, his facial expressions being at once comical and yet sickening.

I saw a client who lived in sheltered accommodation a few times, another nail fetishist, but unusually liked coral coloured nail varnish, maverick! He was also up for some SPH or small penis humiliation, not that common a request, unsurprisingly, shame, as it's very easy and always very appreciated. Involving, as the name suggests, blatantly humiliating a man by laughing at his tiny penis (I find most SPH clients do not actually have tiny penises). Usually, these clients like me to keep telling them they can never satisfy me, they really seem to like that concept. During one session with Mr. sheltered accom, I accidentally pulled his emergency cord, the one that gets you through to matron if you are having a heart attack or in distress. Matron was right on the ball too and buzzed through to the flat, asking what the emergency was...he didn't tell her a visiting hooker had accidentally pulled it when she fell over getting up off the bed, no.

There was a client I saw at quite a posh hotel, German he was. Let us call him 'The cobbler'. He was obsessed with, of all things, frog skin boots! As far as I remember he fantasised about skinning enough frogs for me to make a pair of boots out of the skin, hmm very Vivienne Westwood! Add into the mix that I was pissing on him as he sat in the bath as he rambled on about his froggy friends. Now I have been a vegetarian since 1987 and was, of course deeply conflicted by his non-vegetarian footwear rubbish.........I seem to remember we finished the appointment by him asking me to punch his knob which he had placed on the coffee table, he was on his knees you understand, he hadn't removed it like an ornament. I obliged but went easy on the man, there are laws regarding GBH!

Speaking of frogs. One client enquired if I would hold live frogs during the appointment. Now, by this point I had been doing the job for donkey's years and I knew there would be more to it. A lot of clients who want weirder stuff are very cagey about it and will tell you the tip of the iceberg to test the waters never the full extent, but this Kermit lover had not banked on my vast experience of client bullshit. I asked what he got out of the whole frog thing, he replied that it was to do with the danger of wild animals mixed with sexuality......A FROG???!!! Depends on how big it is I suppose, but I quizzed him more, as I knew there would be more to this crap than he was telling me, he added he would like me to be dressed as either a baby or a Barbie doll, picture the scene! I had no intention of taking the job anyway as like I have said I am a lifelong vegetarian and animal lover (and not in the same way as this dude) and will not involve animals in any way and I would not have been surprised if he had wanted to cum over a frog or some such sick wrenching activity. I declined.

Quite regularly I get requests from prospective slaves to come to my home and clean and be a general dog's body and figure of ridicule. I personally could not think of anything more tedious than having some weirdo skulking around my flat doing my housework all wrong, probably naked with a butt plug hanging out or some such. Over the years I've had many clients who referred to me as Mistress and were my subs (submissives). They would often want to buy me gifts and take me on shopping sprees, a type of financial domination. Not being a fan of shopping, I would dread the shopping spree, sometimes harder than being salivated over for an hour for me, crowded stores, shopping parents and their screaming children are not my favourite things, but my tactic was simply to keep the receipts and return the items.

Some men are into a more basic form of financial domination I called rinsing, although there are other terms for it. This could be a cashpoint meet where I would simply meet the client at a certain cash machine, he would withdraw an agreed amount and give me it. I would treat him with disdain during this meeting. Those clients who like it, love it. Now that is money for nothing!

Another request I get at least twice a year is to be 'kept' by a client, exclusive to him. Like a salaried girlfriend. Once I pointed out my potential earnings (without having to shackle myself to one, let's face it, odd client exclusively) and made them aware they would have to pay me the equivalent (not that I would even consider it, but I'm an argumentative git so couldn't help myself getting into it with them) they would always decide it wasn't such a good idea. I would also point out to them that it was just plain weird and to 'go away'.

CHAPTER 6:

DANGER, DANGER!

I've been asked frequently, 'Aren't you ever scared?' Meaning, scared of meeting unknown men, going to their homes or wherever and my answer is always, 'no'. It is not likely that a potential murderer will book an escort through an agency – too many questions asked; too much of a trail and if he opted to come to the agency flats there were always other girls knocking about. Hotels are covered by CCTV and have security and, we had to text in and out of jobs, at the agency I worked at it was noted if an escort hadn't texted 'out' of an appointment. Once I was an independent escort, I did not have that backup but, honestly if you think sex workers, like me, are constantly fighting off attackers, you are wrong.

As an aside, the laws in this area of sex work actually make it less safe for the sex worker, in the fact that two people working together in the same accommodation classifies it as a brothel and hence illegal, revising this law would at least give the sex worker; a) some security, b) some company and c) potentially support, so, in other words, the laws are not there to benefit sex workers.

There are certain things I do as an escort once I am with the client to assure myself that I am as safe as I can be. I ask the client not to lock his front door if I am at his home. If he doesn't like that idea, I tell him to lock it, but leave the key in the door. Some clients have all their lights off and doors closed in the venue, so I am sometimes expected to walk into the total unknown. There could be five men behind his settee! These clients are always genuinely unaware of how that looks to me; probably trying not to draw the attention of the neighbours.

Most clients are utterly paranoid about their neighbours working out what they are doing, or alternatively trying to create some kind of sexy atmosphere. They offer to put all of the lights on and open all doors once I point out how it can look to me, and most clients are desperate not to come over as dodgy in any way and are usually considerate of these matters.

When I enter the room, we are going to be using for sex I always give it a visual sweep for any open laptops or a briefcase poised on a desk, anything that could be recording, although I understand some cameras can be totally undetectable. I do as much as I can.

I also watch them make a drink for me if one is offered, so they can't slip something into it. I never drink alcohol with a client. Some clients just presume you will – a lot of clients presume we are all 'party girls'. A lot of escorts do take a drink though, but it is a total no-no for me. It doesn't take much booze to possibly make you do something you wouldn't ordinarily, and I always drive to appointments, and I don't touch a drop if I'm driving. I had quite a few clients for whom it was a deal breaker. They would bang on and on and on about it – usually if they had booked me for a longer appointment – a dinner date or whatever. I often wondered if they had never known a woman fuck them sober or they were so crap in bed they thought I'd notice less if I were half cut. Or they could be presuming they would get me to do more outrageous stuff if I'd had a drink. Little did they know, I really didn't need a drink to outrage anyone so, sober it was for Gina!

If I absolutely had to, I would 'fake drink' with these clients, usually because they just would NOT shut up about it. Taking little fake sips and pouring it onto the carpet at opportune moments or spitting it back into the glass when they weren't looking. If there was an open window I could hoy it out of, all the better. Then acting a bit silly and floppy for the duration, hoping the more they drank the more incapable of the act they would be, and I'd get an early finish as they cringed with embarrassment at their inability to perform. Silly what some men will pay for, ain't it?

I heard of escorts at the agency getting blotto with clients, but these were usually the women I could tell had problems, and issues. Actually, that reminds me of one particular escort who had a drinky poos with a client and proceeded to get blind drunk and shat on his living room carpet…quick, someone get the Shake 'n' Vac out! These were the girls generally who would start going out with clients when the clients started giving them the 'You're too good for this, I can take you away from all this, be my girlfriend' crap, or as I call it, 'the I don't want to pay for it anymore' patter. Loads of escorts fell for that one and not just the silly young 'uns, even grown women who you'd think would know better. Surprise, surprise, it usually ended badly, or just ended full stop – hmm, wonder why?

Now, I could be flippant and tell you the biggest danger within escorting is dehydrating and light headedness from all the fake heavy breathing, moaning and orgasms (any heterosexual females reading…let's not pick at that scab, eh ladies?!). And to be honest, a lot of the noises we make are very real, but it is pain rendered to sound like pleasure, as most women will know, having something inserted into you when you aren't in any way in the mood can be extremely painful. But, at the end of the day, that is your job, not a lot you can do.

It is more of a problem with a jumbo-sized cock, admittedly, but not necessarily. I and some other escorts dread massive dicks, too much like hard work. Everything you do with it hurts and they take longer to cum, fact. Nerve endings are more spaced out, I think. If I have a client with a cock so big, I have to use both hands at the same time to wank him, annoying and exhausting! Much better the smaller appendage. I found taking a couple of painkillers about twenty minutes before expected penetration from a client I know to be well-endowed dulled the worst of it.

I did have a client with a cock so small I was dreading him expecting sex; it just wouldn't have gone in! He made do with a 'pinch wank', which was my term for a 'thumb and forefinger only' wanking technique. You have to be careful with that, not (mushroom) for error, get it?!

Back to dangers. A rookie mistake was looking down between your legs when a client was performing oral sex on you. You do not want to see the top of an unknown wrinkly bald head or worse if they happen to look up at the same time and they have spitty crap all around their mouth or worse, in the beard – bleugh! Or clients who fart during oral sex and/or 69s, or possibly giving a blow job to a man who has considerately covered his cock and balls in deodorant and is slowly poisoning you with them. The choking hazard of a male pube lodged in the throat on your drive home is a real one.

Face sitting brings its own issue; - raw fannyitus I think it's called. I once did a face-sitting job (with face sitting the "sitee" usually likes the "sitter" to use their full weight and really grind down on their face) and made a rookie error. I had not checked out the stubble texture! This client was one of those men who have stubble akin to the most rasping sandpaper in the shop. Now, weirdly as I was doing all the grinding, I was fine, was feeling no pain, but the next day I woke up with an untouchable vulva.... ouch! I had to take 3 days off. I took my red raw vulva on a few days' trip to the peak district.

Think my favourite place was Bakewell, yes yes, Bakewell tart, heard it before!
The morning after pain of 'rimmer's tongue', soreness under the tongue where your teeth have scraped that stringy bit under said tongue and general tongue ache from sticking the damn thing out so far. Or almost losing my wristwatch up a lad's arse when I fisted him. God, I don't think he had any innards!

I'm not totally naïve, I realise there are real potential dangers in this type of work, it's just that nothing like that has happened to me; maybe because I am always very professional and lay the law down straight away with clients. I got a reputation at the agency for this, and I know the agency's more potentially dubious clients didn't book me for that reason. They tended to book new girls to the agency and younger escorts – thinking they would be easier to manipulate or try things on with, which they probably were to a greater extent.

I can recall a few clients and bookings that could have gone either way though. The first that comes to mind was a client who, years later, went on to be convicted of rape – not an escort, I might add. I saw his face flash up on the television news and caught the tail end of the report and it made me think back to our appointment. I had seen him once before and yes, he was weird that time but didn't seem like a potential danger. He turned up with an incongruous briefcase making me dubious, and I told him to put it under the bed for the duration. He seemed to have a chip on his shoulder and was rambling a bit. He seemed to be trying to shame me or belittle me, but nothing too blatant and I just put him in his place and got on with the job. I don't think he wanted anything sexual if I remember rightly.

The second time I saw him he had the same kind of thing going on, but a lot more over the top. His attitude straight away was patronising, and erratic, trying to bamboozle me with his pseudo-intellectual babble and 'long words', most of which he was making up. I couldn't get out of him what he wanted to do sex-wise – he kept avoiding the question or again it prompted him to ramble about nothing, random words strung together really. It was extremely boring...either say what you want or leave, was my thinking. But he was starting to get weirder – insisting we sit under the duvet and whisper our conversation. Now you may be thinking 'just chuck him out!' but put yourself in my position. I don't know him, he could turn violent, he could pull a knife. As an escort, a good one anyway, you get very good at reading situations and clients and handling them carefully. I knew one of the other escorts was in the flat, so that was good, but he still needed cautious handling.

I remember at one point he picked up an item of clothing I had removed and as I was explaining to him that his behaviour really wasn't acceptable, he flung it at me. It caught my eye, nothing sharp, but we all know when something catches your eye, it stings like hell. That's where I drew the line, and I told him to leave; that an appointment with an escort was a two-way street and he hadn't upheld his end of the bargain. Oh, God – this sent him off on a tirade about 'fallen women' in his usual babbling non-sensical fashion. All the time I am trying to work out if he is concealing a weapon or what his next move might be. Seeing his face flash up in that news report made me think.

There was another occasion where I was booked by one lad who lived in a big house, obviously a shared house. Maybe five or six other tenants, students maybe. The client was foreign, maybe eastern European, I can't remember for sure. He really didn't speak much English, but enough and we proceeded with the appointment.

After five minutes or so I could hear voices out in the passageway. I asked who else was in the house and did they know not to just barge in. He said they were the other tenants and that they wouldn't bother us, so we carried on.

The whole time I could hear movement outside the door. I had already checked there wasn't a keyhole to peer through!

We had all but finished when there was a knock on the door and a young lad in his early twenties popped his head around. I was sitting on the bed, still mostly naked, so I asked if he would leave until I was dressed. He spoke, but not English, so I was none the wiser, but he did close the door...for about ten seconds.

There was another knock and hey presto, there were about six young men, all talking in a different language, crowding in the doorway. I immediately asked the client to tell them to leave, at the same time getting dressed, but surprise, surprise, his English seemed to have deserted him and they proceeded to discuss something or other in their language.

The client had booked for an hour, but we were done and dusted after thirty minutes, and this arsehole friend seemed to think he could have the remaining half an hour! I worked it out from gestures and the occasional recognisable word. I tried to explain that it didn't work like that, still only half-dressed mind you, and it really wasn't on to have seven men all talking a language I did not understand, heatedly, piled into the room.

The discussion was getting quite animated, and it was then

that the potential of the situation dawned on me; who were these people? They obviously didn't give a shit that they were making me uncomfortable so, now fully dressed and car key between my index and middle finger to be used as an eye gouger if necessary, I just got up and strode as confidently as humanly possible past them all into the hallway with a 'Well, I'm off now, lads'. I quickly headed down the stairs, to the front door – open, thank God – and into my little car and away. I drove around the corner and rang the agency to tell them not to send another escort to that address.

Being flippant once more, I do remember learning very early on that when on top of the client in a 69 it really is best not to look at their feet. There is a gap in the market for anyone out there in reader land for a pedicure product or treatment that targets men – there is a fortune to be made, I am sure. And mix that in with getting a constant whiff of bum crack and the never ending 'press up' position you must hold, cutting off circulation to your hands and its sweet relief when they have done their dirty business and you can flop off and get some feeling back past your wrists again.

On a more serious note, I did have to take a client to court for stalking me. He had booked me maybe three times. He had an odd, nervous demeanour at our first meeting, which I put down to the usual new client nervousness, but I later started to believe, because of a lot of anonymous Facebook messages I had been getting, that he had picked me out much earlier. I had been in a newspaper article about a year earlier, with a photo and my real name and I have reason to believe he had latched onto me then for some reason.

On about the fourth appointment, he asked me out on a date, not as an escort, but an actual date. This does sometimes happen – a client reading the situation wrongly, reading too much into the whole thing just because I was always polite and sensitive, but very clear, that is not the setup here. No discussion. He said he understood and that was that, but another couple of appointments later he started asking again. I refused again and started to think I should stop taking his bookings, for his sake. But again, he said he understood.

Then the bombardment of text and phone calls started. I ended up having to inform the police and got a PIN (police information notice) against him. This meant that if he contacted me again I could have him arrested. He had taken umbrage that I wasn't flattered or grateful that he had asked me out and hadn't fallen at his feet. How DARE I? Clearly, he thought he was such a catch, and I should have been so relieved to have a client such as him, instead of dirty old men. How could I refuse?

It escalated further when one night I got a massive shock – he was going mad on Facebook; creating loads of different profiles and sending vile and threatening messages via them and there it was – a video popped up of us having sex. Yes, he had been filming one or some of our appointments and he now decided to put one on Facebook. I went straight to the police with it all. The thing is, he thought he could threaten me, control me because I couldn't or wouldn't go to the police as I was a sex worker. The police have always been very helpful if ever I have had to go to them for any sex work related issue. I took this man to court and won. When I turned up to court the police officer asked if I wanted to go in through the back entrance just because the client was standing outside having a tab, I said no thank you because I did not need to hide, I think she was surprised as she told me that oftentimes in these cases the woman doesn't turn up. The client pled guilty. I can't remember what the conviction was, but the police had investigated the way they would if this was domestic violence or revenge porn.

There is an unpleasant underbelly to escorting which I can't deny or gloss over. I know for sure that there are unpleasant, dodgy, nasty escorts – the same as there are clients of the same persuasion. There was nasty disrespect from a handful of clients as if escorts weren't real human beings. We were lesser, dirty. Pure misogyny.

I am an independent escort. That is when you don't go through an agency for your bookings; the escort advertises herself, takes her own booking, calls and enquiries. When you work for an agency, you don't see much of that side of things; whoever takes the calls will get it. Plus, the client knows they are just getting through to a call handler when they ring an agency, but when you are independent the client knows they are getting through to the actual escort and that changes their communication considerably.

As an independent handling my own calls and texts, for every normal polite, easy enquiry there are ten total idiots. It's very hard to get across the soul-destroying crap I deal with and ultimately one of the main reasons I wish I could give it up entirely. It saps your will to live to realise there are such morons out there, walking the streets. One could be sitting next to you at work – they are allowed to vote, for God's sake!! All that never made me actually feel dirty or lesser; I know exactly who I am and what I'm worth, but it's just the constant moronic bullshit, drip drip dripping away over time. When you also have many other things going on in your life that may also be going wrong, it is just no way to live. It often drags me down but I suppose the pros are still outweighing the cons.

I admit that I exacerbate the situation as I sometimes can't hold my tongue and reply in a, shall we say, rather sarcastic fashion…and that is really not a road I want to go down – these clients can be vicious and thick as pig muck and I, all of sudden can't make them see the light, can I? It's a shame, they give the many decent, polite clients a bad name.

I often get requests for 'car meets', meaning the appointment would be conducted in the client's or my car – absolutely NO WAY. I have no desire to be driven off into the night never to be seen again, but thanks for the offer. It must've been one desperate/stupid escort who agreed to such meets, for sure. Although, when I was with the agency early on, I did meet a client in an articulated lorry parked in a designated lorry park as many of the agency's other escorts had already been to see him, so he had a safe track record. I was looking forward to getting inside the cab as I had heard some had all mod cons, yes, I do sound easily pleased and I was quite impressed and in awe of his tiny microwave!

Sadly, as an independent, I've had a few requests from clients that were totally unacceptable. Mainly to do with acting out daddy/daughter fantasies or rape fantasies. I have passed some of these details on to the police when I have managed to glean enough information, which, again, the client doesn't expect an escort to do; thinking I wouldn't want to raise my head above the parapet with them. That is because they have a misconception of the law and they think I am doing something illegal already and wouldn't dare go to the police when they ask me to have sex with a dog for example.

What makes me angry about that from my own perspective is some clients seem to think 'Well, she's a prostitute so she will do ANYTHING'. Well, no I won't and only the scummiest or beaten down desperate woman would take those jobs, I say. I am prepared to sell sex for money, consensual sex between adults, that is it. I think the thinking is 'she can't have any morals if she's selling herself'. Well, I don't find a woman selling sex for her own profit immoral.

On a few occasions, I have seen clients when I am out and about, shopping and whatnot. I don't greet him or acknowledge him first, simply because I never know if they are with a partner and if my saying hello would spark the domestic of a lifetime! If they greet me that is fine. They are always discreet, nobody has ever shouted 'Good morning, you big ol' whore' or anything.

The only time I can recall a previous client being a total idiot in this way was when I was out having a meal with family and he and his friends were sitting a few tables away and kept looking over in a stupid over the top way and then started saying my escort name in a stage whisper, pathetic really. At the time my family did not know that I was working as an escort and so could have made a very tricky situation for me. As it turns out, I don't think my family noticed or put two and two together, but that's not the point and it annoys me that some clients seem to think escorts are not just normal people. We have all the same dynamics in our lives that everyone else does, but that's negated by the fact

SEX IS HARD WORK

that you have waved the right by being a slut.

I've had a few clients that thought they could say quite hurtful things or things that could upset or rattle me. Usually things they have found out – or think they have found out – about my private life, presumably online. I find that truly pathetic. They do it to get one-upmanship in every case. Sometimes it is after we've had sex and they've a dawning suspicion that I've been fake, and I was just going to trot off to another client. They had to get a stupid little dig in about whatever they could. Show me, they were better than me. Yawn.

I remember one client making a dig that it said on my profile I was a size 12 (the agency boss would always shave a dress size off for website purposes), but I do have a big arse. I guess he hoped that I'd curl up and die with shame and insecurity. Funny that, because he had been practically drooling over me before we had sex and shaking with nerves. He was putting me in my place because I had seen him vulnerable, I had his money and was off to make more, sex with him didn't matter to me. I can see straight through clients like that, but as I want their cash and as long as it is not so irritating that my head actually explodes, I just get on with it.

It is a different reaction if the client feels guilty. They go quiet and can't get rid of me fast enough!

A lot of the other escorts used to get very nervous about a client being someone they knew. This doesn't bother me, as I don't really know many men or the ones I do, know I am an escort anyway. I don't have a big family of male cousins and uncles, so I know it won't happen to me, but many of the escorts were paranoid about it, especially the Asian girls. Some were from Muslim families and in that culture, there would have been serious consequences if anyone found out they were a working girl.

I do know of one escort who had a booking at one of the agency flats. The buzzer rang, she buzzed him in, and he knocked on the door (probably very faintly, clients always knock so as not to be heard, unless you have your ear pressed to the door, why for,

I do not know). She peered through the spy hole only to be greeted by Pater, Daddy dearest. Hmm, I personally would've wanted to hurl, but there you go. She crept into the living room and rang the agency to sort the awkward incident out and probably ring her mother.   To be more serious though. I did make the biggest mistake of my life and at one point, got onto the other side of the business, running my own escort agency, referred to by law enforcement as a brothel (being on this side of the business has legal consequences) I ran it for a couple of years and made next to no money as it was an extremely hard business to get going for many reasons and running it was one of the most depressing, stressful experiences of my life. You may be thinking that there must be more to say about all this but honestly, I just cannot be bothered to go into it, it was a very boring business to run, (at least men running agencies can perv all the live long day, and in general, do) take my word for it, I wouldn't bore you with the details I ended up being arrested and serving time in prison. I lost everything, my home, my money, some friends, and have a criminal record, not to mention how it affected some family members. I really do not have anything to say about this experience other than I regret it wholeheartedly.

To finish this chapter, I say one last danger in the world of escorting is the smell of a brothel bin. Used condoms, baby wipes and five days of fermentation do not make a pleasant cocktail. DO NOT SNIFF A BIN IN A BROTHEL! Just in case you were ever tempted.

CHAPTER 7

OBSERVATIONS ON THE AVERAGE CLIENT

Main observation: the vast majority of men's egos will not allow them to believe that a woman could be faking or have a totally different motivation for having sex with him, other than lust. A lot of men live in a dream world where women and sex are concerned. I used to get men regularly trying to book me and they would be amazed that I could not remember that I had seen them before……. eight years previously. I also believe most men find the activity more important than the person they are doing said activity with, often sending me a clinical checklist of things they would like to do within our appointment, often with time limits attached e.g.,
1.   two minutes of kissing,
2.   three minutes of fingering,
3.   sex from behind once,
4.   sex with me on top to cum…. twice.

   Etc and so on. It's so detached and passionless. I have asked female friends if they think of sex in that way and they certainly do not. For them it's more about the person and things happening organically.   I usually call what I do 'escorting' as opposed to 'prostitution' – not because I am sniffy about the word prostitute, although I suppose it's the word of choice if someone wants to try to degrade someone for doing this job, but it's mainly just a habit. Saying that, I don't mind the term sex worker; does what it says on the tin, I suppose, but I joined an ESCORT agency, which was the word widely used within the business, but I also use it to highlight a difference in clients' expectations. Yes, it's the same job – selling sex for money, but I think if a client is paying a lot of cash for an appointment, he will have higher expectations from the woman and the experience to someone paying a tenner for a hand job up a back lane.

I also use it to distinguish between my lifestyle, i.e., no drugs, alcohol, violence, being pimped out, that's a life I know nothing about, and the lifestyle of a street walker – putting herself in danger every time she works, working to get her next fix or giving her money earned to a pimp/partner. The words used don't necessarily matter, I can tell if they are being said in a derogatory manner, that's what matters, the intent.

Anyway, what I have noticed is that a lot of people seem to think it's a small band of dirty old perverts who book escorts; men who couldn't get sex any other way, not true. In my estimation, a total guess, I would say 60% of straight men probably see or have seen a female escort. These men are everyman. I and the dozens and dozens of escorts I have known see every single type of man you can think of, from 18 to 85, well off, stony broke, millionaires, ugly buggers, Mr. Average, stunners, fatties, skinnies, pro-athletes, polite, impolite, thick, highly intelligent. I've seen men from every religion; including a catholic priest and all Muslim men think I've never seen another Asian or Muslim man – it's obviously not something they chat about over a cuppa! Indeed, I did sometimes ask clients in general if they ever told anyone in their circle that they saw escorts? They never had, big secret.

I often work Christmas Day, (which I don't mind, I often escort all over Christmas and New Year, as I generally do not celebrate these occasions so find I have time to fill) one year I saw two Hasidic Jews, two Muslims, and a weirdo during the shift. Not everyone has a happy cosy Christmas remember so there is money to be made considering there are not many other sex workers willing to work over yuletide.

Clients are teachers, doctors, the unemployed, students, married, men with girlfriends and the men with boyfriends too, everyone's husband, brother, son, best friend, next door neighbour – all men, in other words. Yes, a handful of dirty old men but hey, what do you expect?

In all my time as an escort, I've only ever had three enquiries from lone women and, to be honest, two sounded deranged. One was talking like a Dalek down the phone and the other sounded like a serial killer; I would imagine, not having a lot of friends who kill serially. If I see a female client she is with her male partner, full stop.

When I see a couple, I have learned to have a chat about dos and don'ts. I find sometimes reality hits; it can occasionally go a bit sour.

I have seen a wife slap her husband in the face halfway through a threesome with me. I made the executive decision to grab my knickers and was out the door in a knickerless flash, early finish, excellent!

I find some men can sometimes be selfish in threesomes, and three-ways are very popular. In the run-up to Christmas, clients would often tell me they were treating themselves to one for the festive season. These rather selfish men would try to control themselves for as long as they could, but when it came down to it, it was all about their cock…how original.

Although many threesomes were the female partners' idea, or they were certainly as enthusiastic as the male partner. I do remember taking one female client aside after a threesome, to talk. I felt she had not been as enthusiastic as she might have been, and picked up tension between the couple, and that could have been for many reasons, but I could tell as the appointment progressed, he was a bit of a bully, overbearing. I had to ball him out as he had ejaculated across my bare backside which STI-wise is a no-no and I had already laid down the rules regarding this issue beforehand, so I was livid. I asked her if she was OK and she didn't have to put up with anything he might be doing, she was clearly upset, but defending this fool, well I'm not a relationship counsellor and I had done my bit.

A lot of clients I can tell presume they are probably one of the very few normal clients I've ever seen, as opposed to the hordes of weirdos. A question I would get asked a lot by clients was 'What's the weirdest request you have had?' They were always after some gossip! To be honest, I can't ever remember, as it just becomes all in a day's work and my mind just goes blank, but I do find men who want a girlfriend experience (GFE) the weirdest, in all honesty. That's something you can't pay for. It's the biggest pile of shite in the world. Now, you can pay for someone to give you a bit of ball busting or stick an electric butt plug up your backside and turn the control up to 'thud', yes, 'thud'. That, I find a lot less weird a thing to pay for.

When I first started, I was quite taken aback by how many men ring an escort the minute their wives' backs are turned. The most common reason they had the house to themselves for a day or two was that 'the wife' had gone to look after a sick mother or had gone away for a break with a friend or had to go into hospital for a night or two. But I have had clients that have booked when their wife had just gone out for the day or the evening. I tell these clients, if I hear a key in the door, I am away – I'm not staying around to have my eyes scratched out.

One client I saw a few times used to book me when his wife had gone to bingo. They were an elderly couple, and he had a fetish for muscular women, always had porn on his tablet showing Amazonian ladies throwing men around. I would give him a fireman's lift all around his living room then squeeze him into submission, his head between my rather powerful thighs until his face went too purple for my liking, or he would tap my leg, the signal to release his bonce and I would ease up.

I have had clients try to book me for a threesome with their wives but have wanted to set it up as if we have all just met on a night out or something. I always refused. I think that's an awful thing to do to someone, sneaky and selfish on the client's part. Everyone has the right to know who they are having sex with, and the wife concerned certainly should have known she was with a sex worker.

In fact, so many clients turn to an escort as soon as they are not their wife's centre of attention, sexually or otherwise, like when their wife is pregnant or menopausal. Don't think of supporting your partner, working on the relationship or anything, no, your sexual needs aren't being met – quick, where's that escort agency number?

This type of 'family man' would sometimes opt to carry out the appointment on one of their kids' beds (broke one once in such a way), so they wouldn't have to suffer the pangs of guilt of shagging a prozzie on the marital bed. Or if that wasn't an option, it was the big old bath towel on the couple's bed. Easy to simply screw up and shove in the washing machine after the appointment, like it never happened. One client did bother to blow up an inflatable mattress for his booking and proceeded to talk about his wife's vagina in the most disgusting way, cheat on your wife with a sex worker if you want but hold back on talking about her like shit to said sex worker maybe?

Many of these men voice the opinion that our appointment is not them cheating, it isn't really cheating with an escort, is it? Tell your wife when she gets back then, dude, and tell her I gave you a blow job without a condom too, she'll love that, I'm sure she would see it in exactly the same way as she puts the dinner on.

It seems that clients think that, as escorts, we can turn down, old, fat, or ugly clients, all the while presuming they are none of these things. Their thinking is, that as I am not a skank type I can pick and choose. Well, yes, within reason, I can. We were never forced to see a client at the agency I was with, but the fact was, the job is what it is, you can't be an escort and wait to only see Brad Pitt types or men you desire – you would be waiting a hell of a long time. I have no idea what a client is going to be like before I clap eyes on him anyway so how could I even operate that policy? It's a practical life, not a sexual one.

A few attitudes I find telling are when clients ask if I have a boyfriend, and I reply 'no'. They then say, 'well I suppose you don't need one, you get enough sex doing this, I suppose'. Now, where do I start? Firstly, in my job I have crap sex with any old Tom, Dick and Harry with cash on the hip, this is not fulfilling my deepest physical needs. Secondly, is all you want from a partner, sex? Or are partners supposed to be friends, companions, the light of your life? Call me old fashioned, but I think they are not just a body to have regular sex with!

Another classic I often come across is this: I was chatting to a client, and we got onto the subject of other escorts he had seen –and the profiles were always of lovely lusty ladies, usually young or youngish, slim or well-shaped, tumbling hair, glamour personified. They booked an appointment and who turned up or opens the door, but Waynetta Slob, or her mother, on a bad day and no, her personality was not making up for it. On getting this part of the story I would simply bide my time until the point where they made it apparent that they still had sex with her anyway – always citing that they thought they might get into trouble otherwise, they could have just left her with the cash if they felt that afraid, Total BS! I just don't think most men have any insight as to why a woman would become a sex worker and cares even less. I have had so many clients telling me stories of meetings with escorts where the woman had necked a whole bottle of prosecco at the start of the booking or seemed 'odd' or displayed some other questionable behaviour, yet they have just got on with the appointment, not seeing it as any of their business or concern. NEWSFLASH: - If a woman, sex worker or not, has to be drunk to have sex with you, they don't really want to have sex with you, but hey, as long he gets sex, who cares right?

One reason many men book an escort is they simply want guaranteed sex. Many clients have opted to pay for sex because it turns out that they see spending money on a date as a precarious investment, a potential waste of money, you see. They pay for the date but they really just wanted sex for that, but unfortunately for these men, women have the right to say no. As does an escort, of course, but unless the man does something outrageously unacceptable, she's not going to. I come across that attitude over and over again, romance, eh? I think this is the main motivation for many a man to book an escort. They don't have to do the boring getting-to-know-you stuff, they don't have to try.

Sometimes it's a power thing, like a top-ranking footballer I was booked by one evening. He took me to a casino and proceeded to throw his copious amounts of cash around and tell people they weren't rich enough to bet against him and wanted me to sit at his shoulder, fawning and looking awestruck. The only thing I was awestruck by was the fact he told me that his plain white T-shirt with a strategically and beautifully placed rip in it had cost £700 or something…what an awesome prat!! He was making such a knob of himself, eventually security was called, and I was off like a shot. TAXI!!!

Sometimes, they book because they like something weird that they will never get without paying someone. In some circumstances it may be simply loneliness. Speaking of money, the boss at the agency would tell us all what to say if a client asked us why we did the job; as they quite often did, to 'never say it's for the money.' I followed that rule for the first few years, coming up with reasons like I love the freedom of it, which of course, I do. The biggest motivation is the potential to earn in an hour what it would take me twelve or thirteen hours to earn in a regular job, but it gets hard to answer that question when you can tell the client wants to hear 'It's because I'm a nympho, sir'.

How many times did I have the presumption levelled at me that we escorts must all be sex mad? Presumably, they can't remember the bit where they give us the cash? I CAN. I am a good enough actress and can bullshit with the best of them, but there are always certain things I just can't bring myself to say, like 'Ooh, I just love sex and can't get enough, MAN!!' That type of stuff doesn't come out. I fudge on that topic or get my tits out – they are well known to distract. I can never get over clients asking what I want to do in the appointment or what I enjoy……erm, we have done that bit already, you paid me. Or maybe I could reply 'anything where your massive saggy belly doesn't keep slapping against me, please'. I mean, look at ME, then look at YOU. Really?

As a rather lucrative side-line, I sell used knickers and stockings and the like. I meet these buyers in my car in a local supermarket car park, very public but nobody is really paying you any attention, lots of coming and going so a good choice for both parties. I let them into the passenger seat and do the handover, always quite surprised they had turned up as knicker buyers are notorious no-shows, hence always meeting in a supermarket only about 5 minutes' drive from my house, not a massive hassle if they stand me up. Anyway, on one occasion the purchaser, a tubby, plain, middle aged bore, got in the car and we exchanged goods for cash, then he enquired about regular late-night meets. I now don't work after 7.30pm so I refused. He, displaying the usual giant male ego presumed it would be because I was scared I was going to fall for him! Now, all I knew about this fella was he was fat, balding, wearing a God-awful anorak and would be back at home in circa 20 minutes (if the bus was on time and he could find his bus pass in all the excitement) with my used knickers over his head wanking.... presuming his mam was out. Not my usual type....

The other great side-line is selling pre-recorded videos and picture galleries of myself on my online profile. I simply dress up in sexy undies and film myself wanking, oiling up my tits, dancing around my sitting room and stripping off. Or more niche activities like pissing or ripping tights off myself, any old crap really, never fails to amaze me what men will spend money on. I also charge a bloody fortune for bespoke videos and video calling, which is very easy money. I did look into Only fans and that type of thing to sell foot and hand fetish content, but I found that only works if you are linked to and are happy to be on social media too and I am not so couldn't be bothered with it really, I find it easier to just stick to what I know.

Further observations: I can never believe how many clients disrobe to reveal some shrunken wrinkled pasty pot-bellied body and present themselves for my swooning in a 'get a load of this' fashion. Now I am all for body confidence, but not delusions. Recalling one appointment many years ago, the client looked the double of Mr. Burns from The Simpsons. I was on top of him, and it was taking ages for him to cum, well, this is what I'm paid for, so I was grinding away, trying not to break his elderly pelvis that is but eventually had to ask, 'have you cum yet?', trying to sound naively curious instead of just bloody annoyed. His reply was

typically ridiculous and went thus 'yes, but I just let you carry on because you looked like you were enjoying yourself so much'......
I literally could have punched him in the face. Oh yes, you are so hot, I love a man who looks like a Halloween decoration! Male ego much?

One more behaviour I simply cannot stand is 'the grabbing'. All the agency flats operate a buzzer system to get in. The client would buzz up and we would press a button to open the main front doors and they would be let into the building. But in one particular flat the door entry button didn't work, so the client would buzz up, but we would have to go down in the lift and bring them back up. Well, some of these men would take the closing of the lift doors as their cue to grab and grope us. The thing is when a client is instantly gropey, it always used to make me a bit panicky, and I know a few of the other escorts felt like that too. I felt like the client was taking away my decision-making time. It's hard to explain. Yes, I was on a website saying I'd have sex for whatever the going rate was and I had seen tons of clients, but when it comes down to it, I am still just me, a woman – a job doesn't override that. It annoys me that they think, 'Right, I've paid for her – I have instant touching rights.'

As an experienced sex worker, you do get inured to a lot of things, but not everything. Now, I don't actually recall walking away from a client just a few minutes into an appointment, but we all have the right to take whatever time it takes to make our own decision, even if it's just ten seconds. If the client starts groping you after five seconds, he is taking that decision out of your hands and that used to make me angry and instinctively panicked. This all happened very quickly and like most things that keep happening, you start to expect it and gain the experience to know how to handle it thinking it will pass, but to this day it still flusters me.

One of the hardest things to do as an escort is to disregard your natural instincts. As I hope you can tell by now from this book, I am strong minded, and I like to think, an intelligent woman and sublimating my natural instincts and subduing my opinions is very hard for me. To not be who I am, i.e., a sarcastic cow, is actually one of the biggest challenges for me. The number of times the client does or says something completely ridiculous or offensive or does something I hate, but like anyone 'at work' I have to keep my mouth shut, nobody is forcing me to do the job and I have a service to provide. Let's face it, if anyone was truly themselves at work, there would be a lot more people getting sacked! For example, quite a few clients will tell me how to lie next to them, what position to assume. I know that sounds weird but honestly, they do...or hold me down in a weird replica of bathing in the afterglow – kind of pin me down and TELL me to relax, never a good way to get someone to actually relax, I find. I personally have a deep hatred of being restricted physically in any way shape or form and this is utter torture for me, I have to pick my battles. Actually, one of the worst things is just lying next to them, head in armpit type thing. When I know they want to 'just lie with me' I get a panic on. Weirdness upon weirdness, lying with some random man as if we had been married for years. I tense up, trying to prop myself up and hold myself in a 'hmm this is lovely and natural' type way, whilst my neck and back is going into spasm.

Quite a few clients try to move my limbs and position me manually, like a rag doll, which is just ridiculous. I always point out that they only have to ask, and I will gladly move my own limbs for them! Even as a seasoned escort I can have awful appointments; ones where my whole body is recoiling at being touched; when it feels like my whole being is screaming NO! My natural instincts as a woman take over and those appointments were upsetting and very lonely, partially because the client had no idea how I was feeling, because I was so adept at my role and because my experience told me that it would all be over soon and I had their money; I would just plough on. I cannot speak for all sex workers, but this is a job you 'end up' doing through circumstance. No little girl dreams of being a prostitute.

You can't just walk out on a client because you are upset or uncomfortable, if it's not his fault. Also, there is money involved, so that always changes any situation; makes things potentially awkward. Some of the worst clients are the bottom feeders, stupid, monosyllabic types who can't string a sentence together who are so thick they can't appreciate they have touching rights of a woman they would never get near in real life, added to that they usually have homes that haven't seen a vacuum cleaner since 2007 and have made zero effort to clean up for me coming round with bedding that is so grubby and stinky I often refuse to lie on it. They always look bemused by this!? It is my job though and I just do my best and count the minutes. I find these jobs quite upsetting though, like I am outside my body looking at myself. A lot of things go through my mind during those appointments, but mainly what the fuck am I doing this for, sadness mixed with anger. As an experienced escort though I know I will move on, and the next client will probably be totally different.

There is nobody to talk to about it either, making it a lonely and isolating job. The few times I tried to explain this type of booking to a non-escort they just did not understand, and I would feel like I was just upsetting and worrying them. This is when an escort needs to have another escort she can talk to, but there is never anyone to talk to, especially once I left the agency and became independent.

It's a cliché in this world that some men 'only want to talk', well they don't – but some talk A LOT. I think in all my time escorting, I've had just one appointment that was all talk. A lot of clients want to talk, but they will always want some type of sex too and the 'my wife doesn't understand me' thing is kind of right, but it's more like 'my wife has gone off sex and instead of trying to work it out together I'm just going to have sex with you'. Within five minutes of the appointment/having sex with clients like this, I always know why their wives no longer want to have sex with them – they are terrible in bed and/or kissing, or they have let themselves go. They are dull as dishwater, or they like to do something weird that is a big turn-off. One thing I do notice is quite a few clients book me because I look like a woman they have just broken up with and are still obsessing over, they never shut up about her. I would see pictures of the happy/unhappy couple around the client's house and surprise surprise, she would look like me. Could be he just has a 'type' I suppose but I think there is a bit more to it most of the time.

Now, I'm sure there are often wives who are causing the lack of marital nookie situations too, but I deal only with the husbands, so I can't comment. I generally get the idea that within a few marriages the wife has sex with the husband until she has the number of children she wants, then that's it, no more sexy time. There is a general lack of understanding of why a woman wants or doesn't want sex. That most women don't just turn on and off like a tap, like most men. I am in no way saying women are perfect or blameless in these situations, but this is a book about my escorting observations.

As I'm sure we all know, sex and performance are a massive deal to most men and often clients will apologise profusely if they can't get it up or are a 'quick draw McGraw', as I call it. The thing is, both situations suit me down to the ground, it means I get a possible early finish – home for 'The One Show', great.

I once had a client find out I had been an escort for 13 years and asked if I had therefore fulfilled all my fantasies? 'Are you on drugs'? Thought I? Now by this point in my escorting career I was hoping to head for retirement (for the 20th time), I had planned to work one last month to milk every penny and then move on, so I had started to drop a lot of the BS and was being.... HONEST! I replied to another man living in a dream world, believing that this job is about the escort's fantasies. I explained that I had a sex life with partners I actually fancied, were my choice and any fantasies would be between me and them. I mean do these people think I'm THAT hard up? Can't they imagine the reality of this mainly gross job? Bizarre.
Once you start this job you can get stuck in a loop, it's difficult to leave.

Another thing a lot, well it seems maybe all men do not understand – if a woman is wet, she must be wet because she is horny. NEWSFLASH TO ALL MEN READING! (Men with wives and girlfriends – I am presuming you are reading this in the shed, am I right?) A woman's vagina can be wet for no reason and most women of childbearing age are wet most of the time to some extent. There is a massive chance it has nothing to do with sexual arousal. Right, that's it, newsflash over. I often used to wonder why no previous partner had ever disabused them of this belief? It is handy though if they think they have made me wet; it adds to their customer experience and it's no effort on my part. Another thing I will never understand, and which actually infuriates me, are clients who try to persuade me to do certain sexual activities. Firstly, and personally, I wouldn't actually enjoy any sexual activity if I have to be repeatedly PERSUADED to do it, would you? Secondly, at times they will do it in such a way as to presume I am a silly woman who is playing coy maybe – needing showing the way and didn't really know what I was talking about. In reality, I am far more experienced than any of my clients – when you have sex for a living that's generally the way of things. I offer or do not offer a particular service for good reasons, which could be a medical reason or some other perfectly good practical motive. That one drives me mad.

Nearly as mad as wondering why a lot of the single men I see as clients do not seem to know that both duvet covers and pillowcases are washable items.

As an escort you see clients with varying levels of experience, but sometimes no experience – the virgin who wants you to teach him the ways of woman and despoil him; quite common in that category is Muslim grooms-to-be, who are petrified of embarrassing themselves on their wedding night. I always remember the look on one young virgin's face after we had sex. I had faked just a believable amount of pleasure for the situation – didn't want to scare the lad – and he started asking questions about how to please a woman in bed. I had to break it to him that all women were different, and he would just have to learn by trial and error. Oh, the sadness, the distress! I think he thought there was one sure-fire way; a magic formula and I as the mistress of the night would reveal it to him – like the secret of eternal youth.

I should have told him one way to please a woman was not to ever wear the God-awful fisherman's jumper he was wearing at the time, in front of one ever again.

The thing is, I don't mean this book to bash clients/men. I do understand they are just human beings getting through their lives as best they can, I try not to judge too much as they, as we all do, will have things motivating them that I was never privy to, but these are honest real observations. Be honest, if I had written a book about all the lovely, polite, considerate, clean, non-weird clients I have seen, you wouldn't have bought it would you?

One such observation is the fact that many clients start our appointment with a big man attitude; defensive, quite unlikeable, but during the course of the booking they change, letting their façade drop and by the end of the appointment are so much nicer once they have relaxed. I just think: 'what a shame you didn't come in like that, it would have all been so much easier', but it's an odd situation for a lot of clients – they are nervous, not themselves – and I understand that.

I suppose you have all heard prozzies refer to 'regulars'? Well, yes, we all have them and by regular we mean someone who may book once a week, fortnightly, monthly or maybe less often, but he's…regular! Once a man has booked me three times, I class him as a regular as a general rule. The regular can be a blessing and a curse, readers. On the one hand, you know they really like you so you can stop trying so hard to come up with 'stuff' (O, how I dreaded clients suggesting that I 'surprise them' if I asked them what they fancied doing sex-wise. God don't make me THINK of sex stuff to do with a man I don't like AND have to actually do it, it really is too much to ask!) so it can be more relaxed. Most appointments with clients I have seen for years are like carbon copies of each other, from the conversation to the room we use for sex, positions, everything. Gets a bit weird sometimes, like a time slip. I sometimes like regulars, you get to know them and can chat with them in a more friend-like way. You get to know about their lives, what they have going on. Like taking candy from a baby.

On the other hand, sometimes these clients, not always,

but sometimes, get a bit weird with you – a bit exasperated that they still have to pay after ten or twenty appointments; like you are being mercenary and selfish. They start to make little digs and snide remarks. I get the feeling they think 'Well, she keeps coming to see me, so therefore we must have something else going on. She must be having the same experience as me'. Yes, I keep coming to see you because you keep booking, Mr. Ego. I must walk a very fine line with these clients. I personally will not exploit clients like these, I know a few other escorts that would though. They let the client think they do actually have feelings for them and proceed to see what they can get out of them. I knew one escort who got a car out of one particularly smitten client. Sometimes these clients would get to the point where they just kept in touch, not actually booking. That was because they obviously wanted me to book them in effect, bit needy but hey, aren't we all sometimes?

For me it is always black and white: business. If and when a client does get overly attached and starts reading far too much into the situation, this often manifests in the dreaded, 'Would you like to go on a date?', I can feel it coming a mile off. I turn them down very clearly. Some clients try that line, thinking they just won't have to pay any more, but I think most who ask are genuine and no matter what the circumstances, if someone plucks up the courage to ask someone out, it's flattering, and I react sensitively. The vast majority of these clients will look a bit embarrassed, but ultimately just take it on the chin. They usually book again and it is all forgotten. Some I don't see again, possibly a little too embarrassed, possibly just found another escort with bigger boobies, don't know?!

To wind up this chapter, I will sum up by saying, against popular opinion, I often feel like I am the one exploiting the client, if anything, not as is commonly thought, that the prostitute is the one being exploited. I know there are many sex workers who are, but that is not MY case. A straight man's need for female flesh and sex, to be found attractive by an attractive woman is extremely exploitable. This is a business where the woman has the upper hand and all the power (or should, if done properly)

Now, I know that's not exactly a massive revelation, but I have to say it. It really is quite breath-taking the way clients buy into my professional façade and God knows, I sometimes test them – say and do ridiculous things; try to see how far I can push it.

You may recall my gyrations with a big ceramic giraffe in an earlier chapter? In general, most men will believe any old shit regarding sex if it flatters their egos and it never fails to amaze me.

Finally, a mention should go to the one client who walked away. I had been working in the business for a couple of years when I had a booking with a man – maybe late twenties, average looking, pleasant, articulate. We chatted and started to have sex, when all of a sudden, he stopped and said, 'This is just stupid, isn't it?' I waited to see where this was going – what his meaning was. He apologised. He hadn't meant to insult, but he had just all of a sudden seen straight through it – saw that I was just doing a job; I didn't fancy him, I wasn't enjoying the sex; I was pretending. He put his clothes back on. I was a little taken aback – never had a man see things for what they actually were, and I thought all the more of him for it but thank God he was the only one – men like that ain't going to pay the bills, are they?!

SEX IS HARD WORK

EPILOGUE

My years of escorting have taught me a lot. It confirms that women have a type of power over men (meaning straight men) that men will never have over women, which many men resent and are scared of, hence misogyny, but all too often we women give our power away to men. I personally refuse to live within the rules and constraints men have set. Men, historically, have not been women's best friends, let's face it.

I heard recently that if men were asked why they feared women they answered they were scared women would laugh at them. When women were asked why they feared men they replied they were scared they would kill them, this illustrates my point. How we as women still live by male standards in a society devised by men for millennia annoys me. Sex does not 'belong' to men, it belongs to both sexes and women are entitled to do with it what they wish, set their own rules. It's theirs to sell if they so desire, to take advantage of and exploit and reap the financial rewards. I don't do shame where sex is concerned.

I have changed quite a lot through my time as an escort. I met a lot of different types of people I would never have encountered otherwise – both other escorts and clients. My eyes were opened, and I had a lot of naivety knocked out of me which, to be honest, I think benefitted me.

I also came to the conclusion that only women should run this type of business and be in charge. I don't think I ever met a man working on the business/organisational side of things who wasn't up to something dubious and seedy, sexually to one extent or another, causing trouble amongst the ranks or, as I would phrase it, 'shitting on their own doorstep'.

The problem is that the man is the customer so escorts using misogynistic language to advertise themselves and pandering to the worst of men's perceptions of women and sex workers, get A LOT of work. It is a business and money talks, the end. I can't see it ever changing. Women should harness their power, but they don't. It is a shame because there is good earning potential in all aspects of sex work, but the social stigma puts a lot of people off. Seldom is the judgement passed on to the consumer of the sex industry.

I am open and honest with people about my job, within reason – I don't tell people at bus stops. I wrote this book because I've not seen a representation of a hooker in the media, film, literature or anywhere else that didn't paint her as a victim – downtrodden, one dimensional, or, at the other extreme, some oversexed nympho who just loves men and is forever sitting in posh hotel lobbies making eyes at stodgy old businessmen, whom she REALLY wants to have sex with. These things are probably all written by men! I was determined, in writing this book, to be painfully honest. I really didn't see the point in writing it otherwise.

Sex workers are just women – your sister, mother, aunty, best friend. I have had dozens of jobs, before and during my time as an escort. Over the years of working in this business, I have become thoroughly sick of it and taken a 'normal' job. Then become thoroughly sick of that and returned to sex work dozens of times.

One thing I have noticed is, people, especially men who know the job I do would think I was referring to escorting/sex with everything I said. For example, I would say 'I have company coming tonight'. I would get a knowing look or smirk, obviously they thought that was code for 'I'm being paid for sexual services tonight'. Well, no, I do have friends like everyone else and one is coming around tonight. Or I might say 'Oh, I am busy this afternoon', the same look and smirk. I think they are thinking 'hmm she will be being paid for sexual services this afternoon', when in reality I might be cleaning my fridge out, doing the weekly shop, popping to my friends for a cuppa or doing my roots. Actually, I find that male acquaintances either just don't talk to me about the job for fear of putting their foot in it I suppose (one said he hadn't read this book for fear of it changing the way he saw me) or they pretend to be very interested in the moral/emotional/political aspects of the job, but they are simply perving, it's very obvious.

I remember mentioning to some clients that I was also volunteering in a charity shop at the time, and they simply could not compute. I find a lot of people, once they know I am a sex worker think my whole life revolves around it, like I never just sit and watch Murder She Wrote or have any other irons in my fire.

On occasions, some people I have spoken to have looked at me with slight horror or pity. I think they presumed I have to do whatever my client bids me to do. I don't. Also, I find that when I tell people the reality of the job, they still think they know better, they seem determined not to listen, probably because they saw a documentary about it 20 years ago, therefore they are an expert, and everybody seems to think it's all other people's husbands, sons, and dads that pay for sex, not theirs. Hmm well it's a booming economy, so who's husbands are these exactly?

I don't think it's necessarily wrong for a person to pay for sex, as long as both parties are getting what they want out of it. A disabled client or someone who for similar reasons cannot go 'on the pull' are a different kettle of fish. But otherwise paying someone to pretend to want to have sex with you is pathetic, and even more pathetic, when they don't even know you are pretending.

I have mixed feelings about the business in general. I don't like to necessarily paint sex workers as victims, we are all different for a start, but don't see myself as a victim. Certainly, I am not always happy or 100% comfortable to be doing the job at times, I am making the best of a bad lot that's all. I'm a big girl and take the responsibility for having chosen and doing the job on my own shoulders for sure but I do have a problem with the fact that men either cannot or choose not to see that most sex workers have probably had problems and sadness in their lives that has led them to do that type of work and use their services anyway. Biting the hand that feeds me and blaming men for booking me is not something I am going to do when I obviously want them to book, it's not that simple. I find it hard to explain how I feel on this point without sounding hypocritical perhaps it stems from my personal feeling that if I ever had the slightest glimmer of doubt that a person I was having sex with wasn't doing it for the same reasons as me, i.e., he or she desired me, I simply could never entertain the idea for one second of continuing to have sex with them. So, it's pretty obvious that when a person asks for financial compensation for having sex with you, they are doing it for that reason, I mean would any of you do your jobs for free? Yet, if men took the same stance as me, I wouldn't have made a single bean. Nothing in life is perfect I suppose.

I would think differently of a partner who had seen prostitutes before I met him. A one-off would be different, but regularly says something very different; he's happy to have sex with someone he hadn't actually seduced or been seduced by. You may find that a double standard, but I don't. I have sold it, not bought it, two very different things done for very different reasons.

I don't worry about what a potential partner would think of my past though – if they can't handle it, they aren't for me, and I can't change it anyway; simple as that. That aspect of the job is not something that has ever played on my mind. I found a way to make money outside of the depressing 9-5 rat race whilst still having loads of free time, that's all.

In fact, I take heart that in this form of sex work, the client/consumer has to see the sex worker as a human being, not just an object, voiceless as is more the case in porn or webcam work, for which I don't blame the woman, as it's men's fault and responsibility if they are capable of viewing a human being in such a way, but I just feel more comfortable doing things the way I do them. I never act dumb and am NEVER voiceless and the client cannot just 'turn me off' once he is done.

I do sometimes have to be circumspect and bite my tongue to best control a situation, I still have all my rights as a woman all the way through the appointment. I have every right to put my foot down and that's what I find most people don't understand or believe.

If there's one thing this still very misogynistic society hates is a woman who 'knows too much' or will not be cowed sexually, hence why there are dozens of derogatory words for a sexually confident, possibly promiscuous, but experienced woman and almost none for her male equivalent. You only have to conjure up the differing connotations of the words prostitute and gigolo.

Being honest, I wish I didn't need to escort. I wish I'd found a fantastic, successful career early on. I didn't, but if I'm anything, I'm hard working and a realist, I don't lose any sleep over it. I do however worry slightly about the legacy. I worry that if I were attacked, or sexually assaulted, heaven forbid, my past could be dragged up to suggest that I was lying, or I deserved it, or was asking for it – as we all know, this is what many people might think. On the health aspect having a lot of sexual partners can give you a greater risk of cervical cancer.

I feel bad that I have worried some people close to me by doing this job too, it has caused arguments and tension with loved ones. Quite a few clients have said to me, 'If I were a woman, I would be an escort, for sure', but it's not that simple – there are implications and issues they don't see or consider because they are men and think it's all about the sex. There are implications for women that wouldn't impact a man.

Quite a few clients want to work as an escort themselves, seeing female clients only, and ask for advice on this, I have to break it to them that not enough women would be interested. We can get sex for free fairly easily and it's just not a woman thing, not enough to pay your mortgage, as you are obviously hoping it will anyway.

Let's face it – most straight men would sell sex to women if enough women would pay for it, but, well, not many would. The thing is, I think a man doing this job would be classed as a stud – there would be kudos, probably be given a medal! As usual, it's different for women.

There are, at times, clients who display a very thin veneer of politeness. I can always sense it straight away. It is a feeling of 'I'll be polite to her cos that's what I'm meant to be, and she might kick up a fuss if I'm not, but she's just a whore and I resent having to be polite to her when I just want to shag her'. I know the veneer would crack pretty quickly in the right circumstances and it did crack a few times and yes, it's very unpleasant, but I have to remember that that was their problem, not mine, and move on. Easier said than done sometimes, admittedly, as it could have been the fiftieth crappy thing to happen that day but, you have to remember, I am not after the client's respect or looking to be made to feel special, that is putting far too much importance on the client. I cannot care less how they feel about me, why would I? They don't have the power to knock my self-esteem. I am after their cash and boy, do I earn it.

Look, sex work obviously isn't for everyone, no way, but then again you could say that about a lot of jobs. In reality, being a sex worker, especially working independently, is just a lot of men contacting you talking total shite wasting your time and expecting you to reply to their texts in a split second because they presume you have nothing better to do, often sending dozens of texts in 10 minutes and other annoying things. There is a lot of sitting around waiting for a job to come in. It's not a job for anyone easily irritated or bored (like all jobs it is very repetitive) …. like me! It didn't take me that long working as an escort to spot a time waster 5 miles off and guard myself against it, but it is just baked into the job unfortunately. As I have said, it can be a very lonely, isolating job as a lot of the time people have no sympathy if you are having a bad day in escorting or something has happened that nobody else would understand or want to hear (I can tell by their faces instantly), but for me it was a valid option – I like the instant money, the autonomy and the freedom it gives me. Although I have wanted to move on for a long time now, hence writing this book hoping something would come of it that would outweigh the benefits that sex work brings me.

Sex work makes me sad, angry, lonely, and isolated and I will be glad to be out it of once and for all. I am not proud of how these emotions sometimes make me act rude and unprofessional with prospective clients making enquiries.

I was also getting sarcastic, one time I had a text from a potential client that ran thus 'bj in a car', now, one of my bugbears was messages from clients which didn't even start with a, 'hi' so this message received the reply '69 in a tractor, your turn' which I thought was very amusing on my part. I couldn't help myself replying to their texts correcting their woeful grammar, punctuation, and spelling.

Can you blame a lass for being desperate for a career change when a potential everyday occurrence is walking into a client's hotel room and it stinking of farts and of someone who hadn't left said room for days. The room was littered with circa 25 beer bottles, cocaine paraphernalia, and general crap. The bed was like Tracy Emins' worst nightmare, yellowy brown stains, the client claimed was spilled Chinese takeaway, but I wasn't risking it, stray bottle tops and who knows what else. The client was worse for wear, unsurprisingly, and I was just bloody sick of being expected to suck someone off in a fog of farts while they talked shit. He presumably expected me not to mind and maybe even get on said dirty bed sheets, I did not. I gave him a blow job, during which I thought he was having an epileptic fit, if I had dentures, they would have been well and truly knocked out! We attempted sex, failed, no surprise there the state he was in, he then decided I had an attitude problem and hurled insults, I exited suggesting he sober up, O yes and I wished him a Merry Christmas….it was December after all. This type of booking was rare, but it was another nail in the coffin.

One totally unexpected consequence of writing this book is that it has been turned into a play, re-titled 'Hard' by local play write, Alison Stanley. I was asked to be part of the cast, as I had previous performing experience. I jumped at the chance and to date, we have performed the play in a couple of local venues as well as a small London theatre, to great reviews. The play is very funny, with some more serious points in there too and is great entertainment, although it has a different tone to this book, if you ever get the chance to see it, do so. However, personally I sometimes found the hilarity of the rest of the cast in rehearsals, laughing at the scenarios and some of the issues of the play, hard to deal with sometimes. I knew their behaviour was never intended to hurt but what they maybe did not know to consider was doing this job was born out of my life not going well, or as I had hoped, disappointment. Nobody forced me to do it but that does not mean it filled me with joy. As I am sure most of you know, people end up doing lots of things because of circumstances, they make the best of a bad job.

To conclude, there is not much I will miss about escorting, I do like being told I am stunning and that my profile pictures don't do me justice and O, how beautiful my eyes are and that I have the most amazing tits they have ever seen (bullshit, I know but it's better than, O God get out, you are gross!) This job can actually be a real ego boost, being told I am beautiful every day. I like playing the femme fatal during the classier bookings and showing off. I like having a lot of free time if I so desire. I will not however miss hearing about men's boring sexual needs all the live long day, having the same conversation with almost every client time after time, being bombarded by emails and texts from idiots, morning, noon, and night and massaging old men's humped, brittle, dry skinned, age-spotted backs and getting covered in spunk regularly. The list could go on and on and on, but it won't so lastly, I will not miss giving any Tom Dick or Harriet access to my genitals and having my bits messed about with. I will be very glad to put them away, only to be brought out on special occasions. All my trials and tribulations have, however, led to me writing this book, which I hope you have enjoyed and maybe has shed some light on a hidden world that is going on right under your nose.

P.S. as I was writing this book, going through probably 10 years of notes I had been making, and I either couldn't remember the story associated with the few cryptic words I had scribbled down at the time, or the story just didn't make it into the book for whatever reason. Anyway, I thought it would be funny to list said notes, thinking you could possibly come up with the full story yourselves, enjoy.

1. Guided masturbation Wednesday.
2. Chastity device and so on.
3. Asian arse hair man.
4. Cold cock/coke can cock/shuttle cock/cock cut in half.
5. Biting an old man.
6. Paint shop strip.
7. Christmas arsehole.
8. Glyndebourne/cheesecake/Eddie Izzard.
9. No arms or legs.
10. Iron filings head.
11. Muslim leader is a French maid.
12. Have you got a hairy arse hole?

THE END

Printed in Great Britain
by Amazon

18160941R00068